CMMI
Complete Self-Assessment Guide

The guidance in this Self-Assessment is based on CMMI best practices and standards in business process architecture, design and quality management. The guidance is also based on the professional judgment of the individual collaborators listed in the Acknowledgments.

Notice of rights

You are licensed to use the Self-Assessment contents in your presentations and materials for internal use and customers without asking us - we are here to help.

All rights reserved for the book itself: this book may not be reproduced or transmitted in any form by any means, electronic, mechanical, photocopying, recording, or otherwise, without the prior written permission of the publisher.

The information in this book is distributed on an "As Is" basis without warranty. While every precaution has been taken in the preparation of he book, neither the author nor the publisher shall have any liability to any person or entity with respect to any loss or damage caused or alleged to be caused directly or indirectly by the instructions contained in this book or by the products described in it.

Trademarks

Many of the designations used by manufacturers and sellers to distinguish their products are claimed as trademarks. Where those designations appear in this book, and the publisher was aware of a trademark claim, the designations appear as requested by the owner of the trademark. All other product names and services identified throughout this book are used in editorial fashion only and for the benefit of such companies with no intention of infringement of the trademark. No such use, or the use of any trade name, is intended to convey endorsement or other affiliation with this book.

Copyright © by The Art of Service
http://theartofservice.com
service@theartofservice.com

Table of Contents

About The Art of Service	7
Included Resources - how to access	7
Purpose of this Self-Assessment	9
How to use the Self-Assessment	10
CMMI Scorecard Example	12
CMMI Scorecard	13
BEGINNING OF THE SELF-ASSESSMENT:	14
CRITERION #1: RECOGNIZE	15
CRITERION #2: DEFINE:	21
CRITERION #3: MEASURE:	38
CRITERION #4: ANALYZE:	48
CRITERION #5: IMPROVE:	65
CRITERION #6: CONTROL:	79
CRITERION #7: SUSTAIN:	92
CMMI and Managing Projects, Criteria for Project Managers:	130
1.0 Initiating Process Group: CMMI	131
1.1 Project Charter: CMMI	133
1.2 Stakeholder Register: CMMI	135
1.3 Stakeholder Analysis Matrix: CMMI	136

2.0 Planning Process Group: CMMI   138

2.1 Project Management Plan: CMMI   140

2.2 Scope Management Plan: CMMI   142

2.3 Requirements Management Plan: CMMI   144

2.4 Requirements Documentation: CMMI   146

2.5 Requirements Traceability Matrix: CMMI   148

2.6 Project Scope Statement: CMMI   150

2.7 Assumption and Constraint Log: CMMI   152

2.8 Work Breakdown Structure: CMMI   154

2.9 WBS Dictionary: CMMI   156

2.10 Schedule Management Plan: CMMI   159

2.11 Activity List: CMMI   161

2.12 Activity Attributes: CMMI   163

2.13 Milestone List: CMMI   165

2.14 Network Diagram: CMMI   167

2.15 Activity Resource Requirements: CMMI   169

2.16 Resource Breakdown Structure: CMMI   170

2.17 Activity Duration Estimates: CMMI   172

2.18 Duration Estimating Worksheet: CMMI   174

2.19 Project Schedule: CMMI — 176

2.20 Cost Management Plan: CMMI — 178

2.21 Activity Cost Estimates: CMMI — 180

2.22 Cost Estimating Worksheet: CMMI — 182

2.23 Cost Baseline: CMMI — 184

2.24 Quality Management Plan: CMMI — 186

2.25 Quality Metrics: CMMI — 188

2.26 Process Improvement Plan: CMMI — 190

2.27 Responsibility Assignment Matrix: CMMI — 192

2.28 Roles and Responsibilities: CMMI — 194

2.29 Human Resource Management Plan: CMMI — 196

2.30 Communications Management Plan: CMMI — 198

2.31 Risk Management Plan: CMMI — 200

2.32 Risk Register: CMMI — 202

2.33 Probability and Impact Assessment: CMMI — 204

2.34 Probability and Impact Matrix: CMMI — 206

2.35 Risk Data Sheet: CMMI — 208

2.36 Procurement Management Plan: CMMI — 210

2.37 Source Selection Criteria: CMMI — 212

2.38 Stakeholder Management Plan: CMMI   214

2.39 Change Management Plan: CMMI   216

3.0 Executing Process Group: CMMI   218

3.1 Team Member Status Report: CMMI   220

3.2 Change Request: CMMI   222

3.3 Change Log: CMMI   224

3.4 Decision Log: CMMI   226

3.5 Quality Audit: CMMI   228

3.6 Team Directory: CMMI   231

3.7 Team Operating Agreement: CMMI   233

3.8 Team Performance Assessment: CMMI   235

3.9 Team Member Performance Assessment: CMMI   237

3.10 Issue Log: CMMI   239

4.0 Monitoring and Controlling Process Group: CMMI   241

4.1 Project Performance Report: CMMI   243

4.2 Variance Analysis: CMMI   245

4.3 Earned Value Status: CMMI   247

4.4 Risk Audit: CMMI   249

4.5 Contractor Status Report: CMMI   251

4.6 Formal Acceptance: CMMI	253
5.0 Closing Process Group: CMMI	255
5.1 Procurement Audit: CMMI	257
5.2 Contract Close-Out: CMMI	260
5.3 Project or Phase Close-Out: CMMI	262
5.4 Lessons Learned: CMMI	264
Index	266

About The Art of Service

The Art of Service, Business Process Architects since 2000, is dedicated to helping stakeholders achieve excellence.

Defining, designing, creating, and implementing a process to solve a stakeholders challenge or meet an objective is the most valuable role... In EVERY group, company, organization and department.

Unless you're talking a one-time, single-use project, there should be a process. Whether that process is managed and implemented by humans, AI, or a combination of the two, it needs to be designed by someone with a complex enough perspective to ask the right questions.

Someone capable of asking the right questions and step back and say, 'What are we really trying to accomplish here? And is there a different way to look at it?'

With The Art of Service's Standard Requirements Self-Assessments, we empower people who can do just that — whether their title is marketer, entrepreneur, manager, salesperson, consultant, Business Process Manager, executive assistant, IT Manager, CIO etc... —they are the people who rule the future. They are people who watch the process as it happens, and ask the right questions to make the process work better.

Contact us when you need any support with this Self-Assessment and any help with templates, blue-prints and examples of standard documents you might need:

http://theartofservice.com
service@theartofservice.com

Included Resources - how to access

Included with your purchase of the book is the CMMI Self-

Assessment Spreadsheet Dashboard which contains all questions and Self-Assessment areas and auto-generates insights, graphs, and project RACI planning - all with examples to get you started right away.

How? Simply send an email to
access@theartofservice.com
with this books' title in the subject to get the CMMI Self Assessment Tool right away.

You will receive the following contents with New and Updated specific criteria:

- The latest quick edition of the book in PDF

- The latest complete edition of the book in PDF, which criteria correspond to the criteria in...

- The Self-Assessment Excel Dashboard, and...

- Example pre-filled Self-Assessment Excel Dashboard to get familiar with results generation

- In-depth specific Checklists covering the topic

- Project management checklists and templates to assist with implementation

INCLUDES LIFETIME SELF ASSESSMENT UPDATES

Every self assessment comes with Lifetime Updates and Lifetime Free Updated Books. Lifetime Updates is an industry-first feature which allows you to receive verified self assessment updates, ensuring you always have the most accurate information at your fingertips.

Get it now- you will be glad you did - do it now, before you forget.

Send an email to **access@theartofservice.com** with this books' title in the subject to get the CMMI Self Assessment Tool right away.

Purpose of this Self-Assessment

This Self-Assessment has been developed to improve understanding of the requirements and elements of CMMI, based on best practices and standards in business process architecture, design and quality management.

It is designed to allow for a rapid Self-Assessment to determine how closely existing management practices and procedures correspond to the elements of the Self-Assessment.

The criteria of requirements and elements of CMMI have been rephrased in the format of a Self-Assessment questionnaire, with a seven-criterion scoring system, as explained in this document.

In this format, even with limited background knowledge of CMMI, a manager can quickly review existing operations to determine how they measure up to the standards. This in turn can serve as the starting point of a 'gap analysis' to identify management tools or system elements that might usefully be implemented in the organization to help improve overall performance.

How to use the Self-Assessment

On the following pages are a series of questions to identify to what extent your CMMI initiative is complete in comparison to the requirements set in standards.

To facilitate answering the questions, there is a space in front of each question to enter a score on a scale of '1' to '5'.

1 Strongly Disagree

2 Disagree

3 Neutral

4 Agree

5 Strongly Agree

Read the question and rate it with the following in front of mind:

**'In my belief,
the answer to this question is clearly defined'.**

There are two ways in which you can choose to interpret this statement;
1. how aware are you that the answer to the question is clearly defined
2. for more in-depth analysis you can choose to gather evidence and confirm the answer to the question. This obviously will take more time, most Self-Assessment users opt for the first way to interpret the question and dig deeper later on based on the outcome of the overall Self-Assessment.

A score of '1' would mean that the answer is not clear at all, where a '5' would mean the answer is crystal clear and defined. Leave emtpy when the question is not applicable or you don't want to answer it, you can skip it without affecting your score. Write your score in the space provided.

After you have responded to all the appropriate statements in each section, compute your average score for that section, using the formula provided, and round to the nearest tenth. Then transfer to the corresponding spoke in the CMMI Scorecard on the second next page of the Self-Assessment.

Your completed CMMI Scorecard will give you a clear presentation of which CMMI areas need attention.

CMMI
Scorecard Example

Example of how the finalized Scorecard can look like:

RECOGNIZE · DEFINE · MEASURE · ANALYZE · IMPROVE · CONTROL · SUSTAIN

CMMI Scorecard

Your Scores:

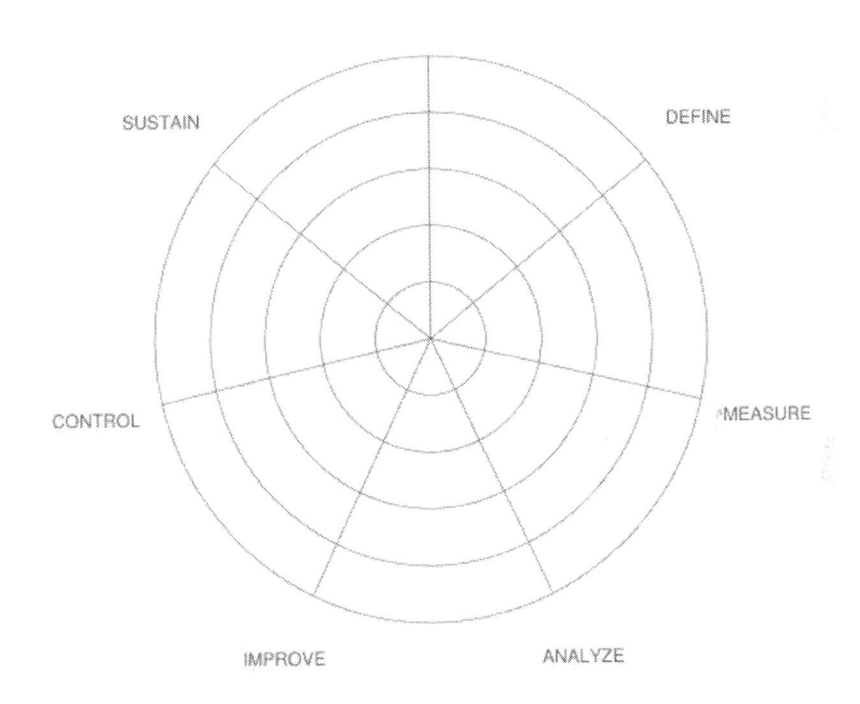

RECOGNIZE
DEFINE
MEASURE
ANALYZE
IMPROVE
CONTROL
SUSTAIN

BEGINNING OF THE SELF-ASSESSMENT:

CRITERION #1: RECOGNIZE

INTENT: Be aware of the need for change. Recognize that there is an unfavorable variation, problem or symptom.

In my belief, the answer to this question is clearly defined:

5 Strongly Agree

4 Agree

3 Neutral

2 Disagree

1 Strongly Disagree

1. How should service sector needs be incorporated into the CMMI product suite?
<--- Score

2. What would happen if CMMI weren't done?
<--- Score

3. Is software quality assurance done by an independently reporting organization

representing the interests of the eventual user?
<--- Score

4. Do you identify the quality trends?
<--- Score

5. How do you know what you need to deliver or do in your project?
<--- Score

6. Which criteria must the team meet before an issue can be marked as resolved?
<--- Score

7. How often do you see requirements that are without problems or schedules that are adequate or management that is sound?
<--- Score

8. What are the expected benefits of CMMI to the stakeholder?
<--- Score

9. What are your expectations with regard to deliverables, if any, that you will need to take with you at the conclusion of your CMMI SCAMPI Class A Appraisal?
<--- Score

10. How good do you need to be?
<--- Score

11. The need for high-quality software is glaring. and what constitutes software quality?
<--- Score

12. Is there an identification of source code level modules with the architecture?
<--- Score

13. Are there test cases identified with each of the requirements?
<--- Score

14. How do you know that whatever was needed to implement requirements was indeed done?
<--- Score

15. Have the roles with associated responsibilities for performing the measurement activities been identified?
<--- Score

16. What is special about Services that it needs a CMMI?
<--- Score

17. What problems are you facing and how do you consider CMMI will circumvent those obstacles?
<--- Score

18. What does CMMI success mean to the stakeholders?
<--- Score

19. Do you need CMMI?
<--- Score

20. Are there any specific expectations or concerns about the CMMI team, CMMI itself?
<--- Score

21. What roles might some not-yet-identified major stakeholders play in service success?
<--- Score

22. What situation(s) led to this CMMI Self Assessment?
<--- Score

23. How do you assess the quality of problem reporting and configuration of software?
<--- Score

24. As a sponsor, customer or management, how important is it to meet goals, objectives?
<--- Score

25. What are the stakeholder objectives to be achieved with CMMI?
<--- Score

26. What do you need to make it a success?
<--- Score

27. What beyond CMMI is needed to help assure program and project success?
<--- Score

28. How are the CMMI's objectives aligned to the group's overall stakeholder strategy?
<--- Score

29. Why do you need Maturity?
<--- Score

30. What factors, as identified in the CMMI literature and case studies, inhibit maturity levels?

<--- Score

31. Who else hopes to benefit from it?
<--- Score

32. How are you going to measure success?
<--- Score

33. What beneficiary-level or social barriers prevented program success?
<--- Score

34. If CMMI were no longer your organization need, would you keep doing training the same way?
<--- Score

35. Is it essential that a CMMI appraisal and an ISO 9000 audit be independent events (and investments) within your organization that is working to meet the requirements of both?
<--- Score

36. How much CMMI-svc do you need for ISO 20000?
<--- Score

37. How much are sponsors, customers, partners, stakeholders involved in CMMI? In other words, what are the risks, if CMMI does not deliver successfully?
<--- Score

38. Which projects will need to be assessed?
<--- Score

**39. Does your organization anticipate any provider

contracting issues in the near future?
<--- Score

Add up total points for this section:
_ _ _ _ _ = Total points for this section

Divided by: _ _ _ _ _ _ (number of statements answered) = _ _ _ _ _ _
Average score for this section

Transfer your score to the CMMI Index at the beginning of the Self-Assessment.

CRITERION #2: DEFINE:

INTENT: Formulate the stakeholder problem. Define the problem, needs and objectives.

In my belief, the answer to this question is clearly defined:

5 Strongly Agree

4 Agree

3 Neutral

2 Disagree

1 Strongly Disagree

1. Are the requirements changes logged and tracked?
<--- Score

2. What are the staff and equipment requirements?
<--- Score

3. How confident are you about the design meeting safety requirements?

<--- Score

4. How is software quality defined?
<--- Score

5. How do you obtain the requirements/requests?
<--- Score

6. What do requirements look like under Agile?
<--- Score

7. How did the CMMI manager receive input to the development of a CMMI improvement plan and the estimated completion dates/times of each activity?
<--- Score

8. Did you meet the requirements specification?
<--- Score

9. Do you meet compliance requirements?
<--- Score

10. Does managing requirements pay off?
<--- Score

11. Place measurement within the context of CMM or CMM within the context of measurement?
<--- Score

12. How confident are you that the product will meet its safety/security requirements?
<--- Score

13. Does product defect tracking begin no later than requirements specifications?
<--- Score

14. When you find an inconsistency that relates to requirements, what do you do to determine and record why it happened?
<--- Score

15. Are different versions of process maps needed to account for the different types of inputs?
<--- Score

16. Does the model behave correctly with respect to corresponding requirements?
<--- Score

17. Does the review address the linking between requirements and architecture?
<--- Score

18. Is a fully trained team formed, supported, and committed to work on the CMMI improvements?
<--- Score

19. Has a high-level 'as is' process map been completed, verified and validated?
<--- Score

20. Have the customer needs been translated into specific, measurable requirements? How?
<--- Score

21. Is a software product used to assist in managing requirements?
<--- Score

22. Will team members perform CMMI work when assigned and in a timely fashion?

<--- Score

23. Has a project plan, Gantt chart, or similar been developed/completed?
<--- Score

24. What are the dynamics of the communication plan?
<--- Score

25. Is the current 'as is' process being followed? If not, what are the discrepancies?
<--- Score

26. Is CMMI linked to key stakeholder goals and objectives?
<--- Score

27. Do you define the quality attributes expected in the product?
<--- Score

28. Which examples of requirements traceability are adequate?
<--- Score

29. Are team charters developed?
<--- Score

30. Has the verification been performed on an already stable version of the requirements?
<--- Score

31. Are formal deliverable inspections performed, beginning with requirements specifications?
<--- Score

32. What are the current program requirements?
<--- Score

33. Is there a critical path to deliver CMMI results?
<--- Score

34. Are you meeting your customer requirements and is your customer happy?
<--- Score

35. Are there any constraints known that bear on the ability to perform CMMI work? How is the team addressing them?
<--- Score

36. Is the supplier by purchase order and/or other agreements required to establish and implement a software quality assurance program?
<--- Score

37. What customer feedback methods were used to solicit their input?
<--- Score

38. Are the requirements sufficient?
<--- Score

39. How can you reduce duplicate test cases in a project?
<--- Score

40. Does the review address the completeness of the requirements?
<--- Score

41. Is the team formed and are team leaders (Coaches and Management Leads) assigned?
<--- Score

42. How often are the team meetings?
<--- Score

43. Are stakeholder processes mapped?
<--- Score

44. Are users involved throughout the project, especially in requirements specification and testing?
<--- Score

45. Which techniques are used in your organization to model the customer requirements?
<--- Score

46. Are you constrained by security requirements?
<--- Score

47. Does evidence exist that requirements have been considered within the project team?
<--- Score

48. Does the review address the comprehensibility of the requirements?
<--- Score

49. Are requirements versus constraints balanced?
<--- Score

50. How do you know that your team is able to implement the new set of requirements?

<--- Score

51. How do you make sure your code implements all the requirements / requests?
<--- Score

52. Do you determine the continuing resource requirements?
<--- Score

53. Has everyone on the team, including the team leaders, been properly trained?
<--- Score

54. How does the CMMI manager ensure against scope creep?
<--- Score

55. How do you know that your team is able to implement the requirements?
<--- Score

56. Does the requirement review cover all requirements (at least the new ones for a release)?
<--- Score

57. Is full participation by members in regularly held team meetings guaranteed?
<--- Score

58. Do you provide double-sided traceability on the requirements?
<--- Score

59. Is there a completed SIPOC representation, describing the Suppliers, Inputs, Process, Outputs, and

Customers?
<--- Score

60. When is/was the CMMI start date?
<--- Score

61. Has the CMMI work been fairly and/or equitably divided and delegated among team members who are qualified and capable to perform the work? Has everyone contributed?
<--- Score

62. Is there a completed, verified, and validated high-level 'as is' (not 'should be' or 'could be') stakeholder process map?
<--- Score

63. Do you place measurements within the context of CMMI or CMMI within the context of measurements?
<--- Score

64. How is the team tracking and documenting its work?
<--- Score

65. What key stakeholder process output measure(s) does CMMI leverage and how?
<--- Score

66. Has/have the customer(s) been identified?
<--- Score

67. In this context of Project Management, what can you say about Scrum alignment with CMM?
<--- Score

68. What are the Roles and Responsibilities for each team member and its leadership? Where is this documented?
<--- Score

69. Has a team charter been developed and communicated?
<--- Score

70. Is the CMMI scope manageable?
<--- Score

71. Do you define the project lifecycle depending on the domain of requirements, the nature of the project, and the estimated resources for the project?
<--- Score

72. What does the quality parameter fitness of purpose mean in the context of software products?
<--- Score

73. What critical content must be communicated – who, what, when, where, and how?
<--- Score

74. Does scrum fulfill the project management requirements of CMMI maturity levels two to five?
<--- Score

75. Are there different segments of customers?
<--- Score

76. How do you keep key subject matter experts in

the loop?
<--- Score

77. Is the team adequately staffed with the desired cross-functionality? If not, what additional resources are available to the team?
<--- Score

78. In this context of Project Management, what do you do about Scrum alignment with CMMI?
<--- Score

79. Which techniques are used in your organization to model the product requirements?
<--- Score

80. Is CMMI currently on schedule according to the plan?
<--- Score

81. Creating software requires keeping track of lots of information. What requirements must the software meet?
<--- Score

82. Are performance or quality requirements required for safety software application?
<--- Score

83. Has the direction changed at all during the course of CMMI? If so, when did it change and why?
<--- Score

84. How do you know that the project team members are committed to implement the current set of requirements?

<--- Score

85. How can stakeholders who are responsible for the definition of requirements take a structured approach?
<--- Score

86. How to interpret CMMI in an Agile context?
<--- Score

87. Is there a CMMI management charter, including stakeholder case, problem and goal statements, scope, milestones, roles and responsibilities, communication plan?
<--- Score

88. When is a structured walkthrough (swt) required?
<--- Score

89. How will the CMMI team and the group measure complete success of CMMI?
<--- Score

90. What rule(s) or criteria do you use to determine the source of your requirements?
<--- Score

91. Is the team equipped with available and reliable resources?
<--- Score

92. Has anyone else (internal or external to the group) attempted to solve this problem or a similar one before? If so, what knowledge can be leveraged from these previous efforts?

<--- Score

93. Has the improvement team collected the 'voice of the customer' (obtained feedback – qualitative and quantitative)?
<--- Score

94. Are you interested in the number of defects associated to the requirements?
<--- Score

95. What activities and milestones were required to launch the initiative?
<--- Score

96. How does your organization manage customer requirements?
<--- Score

97. How was the 'as is' process map developed, reviewed, verified and validated?
<--- Score

98. What is the key effort required for CMMI implementation?
<--- Score

99. Is a role defined that is responsible for customer information?
<--- Score

100. Is data collected and displayed to better understand customer(s) critical needs and requirements.
<--- Score

101. What constraints exist that might impact the team?
<--- Score

102. How will variation in the actual durations of each activity be dealt with to ensure that the expected CMMI results are met?
<--- Score

103. What are the rough order estimates on cost savings/opportunities that CMMI brings?
<--- Score

104. What support is required for a formal CMMI appraisal?
<--- Score

105. What do you do to ensure that project team members are kept current with changes in requirements?
<--- Score

106. Which is used to indicate that the software has met a defined quality level and is ready for mass distribution either by electronic means or by physical media?
<--- Score

107. Do you require your project management practices to be applied at this level?
<--- Score

108. Are improvement team members fully trained on CMMI?
<--- Score

109. If substitutes have been appointed, have they been briefed on the CMMI goals and received regular communications as to the progress to date?
<--- Score

110. Have requirements changed due to something discovered during the sprint?
<--- Score

111. Is a mechanism used for controlling changes to the software requirements?
<--- Score

112. Do you use prototyping in the early stages of the project to validate the requirements/design?
<--- Score

113. Who are the CMMI improvement team members, including Management Leads and Coaches?
<--- Score

114. Do you determine staffing requirements of the project?
<--- Score

115. Do the problem and goal statements meet the SMART criteria (specific, measurable, attainable, relevant, and time-bound)?
<--- Score

116. Is the team sponsored by a champion or stakeholder leader?
<--- Score

117. What are your business requirements for System and Software Assurance?

<--- Score

118. When is the estimated completion date?
<--- Score

119. What specifically is meant by the requirements of the SOW, and SOW element?
<--- Score

120. How much more expensive is it to change in the production stage than the requirements stage?
<--- Score

121. What federal or other program requirements promoted successful implementation?
<--- Score

122. When are you required to submit the Performance Client Questionnaires to your Clients?
<--- Score

123. What are the compelling stakeholder reasons for embarking on CMMI?
<--- Score

124. Which requirements validation methods are used in your organization?
<--- Score

125. Describe the scope of the project; what will it accomplish?
<--- Score

126. Are information security requirements and

requirement changes complete and accurate?
<--- Score

127. Will team members regularly document their CMMI work?
<--- Score

128. What would be the goal or target for a CMMI's improvement team?
<--- Score

129. Does the team have regular meetings?
<--- Score

130. When are meeting minutes sent out? Who is on the distribution list?
<--- Score

131. What are the requirements for system recovery from a failure?
<--- Score

132. Are customer(s) identified and segmented according to their different needs and requirements?
<--- Score

133. What are the main techniques used to prioritize requirements?
<--- Score

134. Is the improvement team aware of the different versions of a process: what they think it is vs. what it actually is vs. what it should be vs. what it could be?
<--- Score

135. What specifically is the problem? Where does it

occur? When does it occur? What is its extent?
<--- Score

136. What are the boundaries of the scope? What is in bounds and what is not? What is the start point? What is the stop point?
<--- Score

137. Are customers identified and high impact areas defined?
<--- Score

138. Is there regularly 100% attendance at the team meetings? If not, have appointed substitutes attended to preserve cross-functionality and full representation?
<--- Score

Add up total points for this section:
_____ = Total points for this section

Divided by: _____ (number of statements answered) = _____
Average score for this section

Transfer your score to the CMMI Index at the beginning of the Self-Assessment.

CRITERION #3: MEASURE:

INTENT: Gather the correct data. Measure the current performance and evolution of the situation.

In my belief, the answer to this question is clearly defined:

5 Strongly Agree

4 Agree

3 Neutral

2 Disagree

1 Strongly Disagree

1. What are the critical success factors you use to measure your software quality?
<--- Score

2. Is there a Performance Baseline?
<--- Score

3. Is data collected on key measures that were identified?

<--- Score

4. Who participated in the data collection for measurements?
<--- Score

5. What impact has the adoption of CMMI had on criteria in terms of intangible benefits?
<--- Score

6. How is software quality measured?
<--- Score

7. What is the sequence of activities in software process performance analysis?
<--- Score

8. How do you measure quality costs on a real time basis in software?
<--- Score

9. What particular quality tools did the team find helpful in establishing measurements?
<--- Score

10. Do you provide quality measures for both individual providers and facilities?
<--- Score

11. Have the risks been analyzed?
<--- Score

12. What is the purpose of quality analysis and evaluation in software design?
<--- Score

13. How much are you spending today on the cost of poor-quality software in your organization?
<--- Score

14. Why focus on process ?
<--- Score

15. Is long term and short term variability accounted for?
<--- Score

16. What is it about your potential user base that will impact the design?
<--- Score

17. What do you measure and why?
<--- Score

18. How would you describe the critical success factors you use to measure your software quality?
<--- Score

19. Are any new tools required for data collection, analysis, reporting etc.?
<--- Score

20. How do you measure software quality?
<--- Score

21. What impact has the adoption of CMMI had on criteria in terms of tangible benefits?
<--- Score

22. What are the agreed upon definitions of the high impact areas, defect(s), unit(s), and opportunities that will figure into the process capability metrics?

<--- Score

23. What are the root causes of problems within the process?
<--- Score

24. What will it cost your organization?
<--- Score

25. Random variation, or special cause ?
<--- Score

26. Agile meets CMM: culture clash or common cause?
<--- Score

27. What are the measures of software quality?
<--- Score

28. How do you measure CMMI Compliance?
<--- Score

29. How do you measure customer service?
<--- Score

30. What is the total cost of quality problems (reworking)?
<--- Score

31. Are key measures identified and agreed upon?
<--- Score

32. What has the team done to assure the stability and accuracy of the measurement process?
<--- Score

33. How do your practices most effectively move the needle against corresponding pitfalls of cost and quality?
<--- Score

34. Does the analysis skills of existing personnel equal or exceed the already stated required by each derived measure?
<--- Score

35. Are base measure aggregation structures compatible?
<--- Score

36. Is data collection planned and executed?
<--- Score

37. How will practices know when the quality measures change?
<--- Score

38. Is a solid data collection plan established that includes measurement systems analysis?
<--- Score

39. How do you ensure software quality in a cost effective way?
<--- Score

40. If you do not implement measurement, what existing challenges will persist?
<--- Score

41. What improvement actions correct the root causes to meet customer requirements?
<--- Score

42. Is the information you capture critical or are you just filling out the template, because you believe that you have to?
<--- Score

43. What impact has the adoption of CMMI had on criteria in terms of tangible costs?
<--- Score

44. What if analytics drove the information architecture development?
<--- Score

45. Is key measure data collection planned and executed, process variation displayed and communicated and performance baselined?
<--- Score

46. Are you within your cost variance parameters?
<--- Score

47. How does your organization reduce the costs of software quality?
<--- Score

48. How do you measure the performance of your applications in the cloud?
<--- Score

49. What are the activities necessary to execute a software process performance analysis?
<--- Score

50. Are process variation components displayed/ communicated using suitable charts, graphs, plots?

<--- Score

51. What is your measure for determining if the quality of the software is degrading?
<--- Score

52. Do you have good measures for behavioral health that facilitate the theme of integration?
<--- Score

53. What data was collected (past, present, future/ongoing)?
<--- Score

54. Do the project measures accurately and objectively represent the quality of the software products?
<--- Score

55. How is business intelligence and analytics impacting the CFO function?
<--- Score

56. Is Process Variation Displayed/Communicated?
<--- Score

57. What are the major business drivers causing your organization to focus on business process change?
<--- Score

58. What is the cost of poor-quality software in your organization?
<--- Score

59. Are the levels and focus right for TOGAF

enterprise architecture?
<--- Score

60. Does the model implementation lead to changes in service utilization patterns and reduced costs?
<--- Score

61. How do you know the impact of requirements changes on stakeholders who are external to the project team, as the customer?
<--- Score

62. Communication: what has been measured, how was it measured, what are the units of measure, and what has been included or excluded?
<--- Score

63. Which methods are used to analyze the derived measures?
<--- Score

64. How large is the gap between current performance and the customer-specified (goal) performance?
<--- Score

65. What are warning signs for long term outcome measures?
<--- Score

66. What impact has the adoption of CMMI had on criteria in terms of intangible costs?
<--- Score

67. What key measures identified indicate the

performance of the stakeholder process?
<--- Score

68. What are the key input variables? What are the key process variables? What are the key output variables?
<--- Score

69. What charts has the team used to display the components of variation in the process?
<--- Score

70. Which maturity is being measured?
<--- Score

71. Which quality measures should you use?
<--- Score

72. Was a data collection plan established?
<--- Score

73. What are the main techniques to analyze the risk of requirements?
<--- Score

74. Does the size or duration of the project have an impact on the way you would implement Requirements Management?
<--- Score

75. Are high impact defects defined and identified in the stakeholder process?
<--- Score

76. How are your investments in good software quality affecting your overall costs of quality and cost of ownership for software assets?

<--- Score

77. How will distributed and collaborative development environments impact the design, productivity, and quality of software?
<--- Score

78. Have you found any 'ground fruit' or 'low-hanging fruit' for immediate remedies to the gap in performance?
<--- Score

79. Will the rapidly growing demands made of new software packages cause a decline in achievable software quality?
<--- Score

Add up total points for this section:
_____ = Total points for this section

Divided by: _____ (number of statements answered) = _____
Average score for this section

Transfer your score to the CMMI Index at the beginning of the Self-Assessment.

CRITERION #4: ANALYZE:

INTENT: Analyze causes, assumptions and hypotheses.

In my belief, the answer to this question is clearly defined:

5 Strongly Agree

4 Agree

3 Neutral

2 Disagree

1 Strongly Disagree

1. How do you test your process without adding more process?
<--- Score

2. What are the requirements for the process?
<--- Score

3. Why acquisition process is necessary?
<--- Score

4. How do you implement the various process areas into your organization?
<--- Score

5. How does process performance change when other observable factors change?
<--- Score

6. What do you do when you do not have enough projects using the process you want to test?
<--- Score

7. Are process improvement programs in place to maintain processes?
<--- Score

8. How long will it take to execute a process?
<--- Score

9. Do software tools support the process activities?
<--- Score

10. Is the process well positioned so that one feels comfortable, is performant and controlled?
<--- Score

11. What does it take to establish credibility for doing process performance?
<--- Score

12. What agile methodologies combined with software process improvement maturity models crafted for small and medium enterprises exist?
<--- Score

13. Can you account for the process areas?
<--- Score

14. Why base your organizations process improvement success on the CMMI?
<--- Score

15. What project conditions and process would offer the best results?
<--- Score

16. Can CMMI be harmonized with other continuous process improvement efforts?
<--- Score

17. What is the difference between a Process and a Procedure?
<--- Score

18. Does the process make it easier for daily work or not?
<--- Score

19. Do the definitions supports continuous process improvement?
<--- Score

20. What is the difference between process metrics and product metrics?
<--- Score

21. Are the product development activities separate from process improvement activities?
<--- Score

22. What exactly makes up a process?

<--- Score

23. Are there breakthrough concepts that you can apply to overall process improvement?
<--- Score

24. Which results should be achieved by the process?
<--- Score

25. Do the appraisal findings declare any process areas non applicable?
<--- Score

26. How would you characterize your organizations dominant process methodology?
<--- Score

27. Has requirements traceability been maintained from a requirement to its derived requirements and its allocation to functions, objects, people, processes, and work products?
<--- Score

28. Can your organization-wide process landscape be established in which the coordination of cross-unit activities is a prerequisite?
<--- Score

29. Does it matter for business process maturity?
<--- Score

30. Is the process capable of meeting requirements?
<--- Score

31. Has the process description been defined and documented?
<--- Score

32. What process suggestions do you make?
<--- Score

33. What is the scope of the business process?
<--- Score

34. Why do you need process documentation?
<--- Score

35. How does your organization use CMMI to improve internal processes?
<--- Score

36. What are the components in the process areas and the relationships?
<--- Score

37. Why improve the software process?
<--- Score

38. Can you measure process activities?
<--- Score

39. To be CMMI compliant, do you need to validate your processes?
<--- Score

40. Does everyone know the why of the process?
<--- Score

41. Why launch a CMMI based process improvement program?

<--- Score

42. Does the CMMI provide explicit support for improving software maintenance processes?
<--- Score

43. Is partial implementation of the proposed process changes possible?
<--- Score

44. How is CMMI different from other process reference models?
<--- Score

45. Is the supplier teams development process defined and being implemented?
<--- Score

46. Is the process finishing with clear result?
<--- Score

47. Is the process effective?
<--- Score

48. What are the components (activities) of the process; what is involved?
<--- Score

49. Is a process defined that feeds new bugs into the hot-fix process?
<--- Score

50. What are the various process areas and goals in the CMMI model?
<--- Score

51. Are process improvement programs in place?
<--- Score

52. Do you consistently manage and perform your requirements development and management processes, and do you have an objective way to control and improve corresponding processes?
<--- Score

53. How do you address the assurance implications of your CMMI-compliant processes?
<--- Score

54. How safe/ secure will the product be as-operated, as assessed during the development process?
<--- Score

55. Which process areas were included in the appraisal?
<--- Score

56. Are managers trained to do process redesign and to manage processes?
<--- Score

57. Does process pilot testing create too much overhead?
<--- Score

58. What are the control levers on the safety/ security process?
<--- Score

59. Can you account for the concept of process area in CMMI?

<--- Score

60. Are there process and product checks throughout the lifecycle?
<--- Score

61. How important is stability of the surrounding context to sustain process maturity and process capability?
<--- Score

62. Is process improvement a good investment ?
<--- Score

63. Do the appraisal findings declare any process areas not applicable?
<--- Score

64. How good are you typically in process X today?
<--- Score

65. What characterizes the current process and performance metrics, and how has it changed over-time?
<--- Score

66. Why create a separate process area for measurement in the CMMI?
<--- Score

67. Are process models defined for the major value chains in your organization?
<--- Score

68. Does the staff have the resources needed to execute the process?

<--- Score

69. Will practices be able to choose track during the application process?
<--- Score

70. Will the process change improve project performance?
<--- Score

71. Which business process maturity model best fits your organization?
<--- Score

72. What is the importance of each activity in the process?
<--- Score

73. Does your organization have a group (or center of excellence) responsible for Business Process Management and, if so, where is it located within your organization?
<--- Score

74. Are you reviewing the status of the activities of the process or the process itself?
<--- Score

75. Is there known benefit from Service-specific process improvement?
<--- Score

76. How many people are directly involved in the risk management process?
<--- Score

77. Can the process go on despite unexpected problems?
<--- Score

78. What is the review process for Vendor provided tools?
<--- Score

79. Is there an architecture management process described?
<--- Score

80. Is the traceability of requirements verified in a review process?
<--- Score

81. What are your organizations process improvement needs ?
<--- Score

82. Does your organization have process managers who are responsible for processes?
<--- Score

83. How do you develop measures of performance in your Process Areas, associated with the generic and specific goals and practices?
<--- Score

84. Do some groups want to independently improve and measure process improvement?
<--- Score

85. What is the process to fix an ineffective process?
<--- Score

86. Can the process be adjusted?
<--- Score

87. Do you determine the process requirements for each activity in the project?
<--- Score

88. Does everyone know how they fit into the process and what to do?
<--- Score

89. Why is process maturity important?
<--- Score

90. How much process improvement experience do the various units within your organization have?
<--- Score

91. Are the activities and work products listed in the processes visible?
<--- Score

92. Have your practitioners been trained in your review process and software?
<--- Score

93. How do you define process?
<--- Score

94. Does the right process or procedure exist?
<--- Score

95. Is the process understandable for people who use it?

<--- Score

96. Which tools are needed to execute the process?
<--- Score

97. Are there additional methods you would include in the software assurance process?
<--- Score

98. Does your organization implement a process architecture towards lean in product development?
<--- Score

99. Which parts of a particular process that should be improved?
<--- Score

100. Are there part process owners which act as an owner and are responsible for sub-processes?
<--- Score

101. What can be done to more effectively coordinate work with the suppliers CMM/CMMI processes?
<--- Score

102. What should be your first process to document?
<--- Score

103. How does CMMI process improvement affect software developers?
<--- Score

**104. Do your assurance processes meet your

business requirements?
<--- Score

105. Is there a common industry-wide approach or is each following its own process?
<--- Score

106. Do you use CMMI-svc process areas to answer questions?
<--- Score

107. How and when is the process evaluated?
<--- Score

108. How can the CMMI Validation process area be used to make pair programming more robust?
<--- Score

109. Is the documented process what you actually do?
<--- Score

110. To what degree are IT Governance, process and quality frameworks in use in your organization?
<--- Score

111. How are your job duties related to your organizations software assurance process?
<--- Score

112. Is there your organizational software configuration management process?
<--- Score

**113. Can the process continue in spite of

unexpected problems?
<--- Score

114. What process has been implemented, how does it work and what are its key elements?
<--- Score

115. What quality assurance processes are followed before releasing software patches?
<--- Score

116. What would you change in the presented process?
<--- Score

117. What is the escalation path and process for problem resolution?
<--- Score

118. Is there an escalation process defined?
<--- Score

119. Can people CMM adoption significantly improve the capability of CMMI process areas?
<--- Score

120. Does staff appreciate formal inspection process?
<--- Score

121. How fast can the process of delivering a system from a given specification be completed?
<--- Score

122. How do you address the stock implications of your CMMI-compliant processes?

<--- Score

123. Are process improvement programs in place to identify and improve problems and defects?
<--- Score

124. How much more could be saved if you found bugs earlier in the development process?
<--- Score

125. Are process definitions compatible with CMM definitions?
<--- Score

126. What process phases and activities is the assessment method made up of?
<--- Score

127. How do you evaluate different process areas within your organization?
<--- Score

128. Is the process designed to avoid errors before they result in product errors?
<--- Score

129. What needs to be done to achieve the set goals without falling into the common every day process pitfalls?
<--- Score

130. What can you (Quality) do to improve the process and help prevent Software bugs ?
<--- Score

131. Will your software community find the

increase in the number of engineering process areas and practices helpful or burdensome?
<--- Score

132. How do you know if the process works?
<--- Score

133. Does software process ambidexterity lead to better software project performance?
<--- Score

134. Can you identify next-generation process improvement methodology?
<--- Score

135. Do you record process and product quality assurance activities in suitable detail?
<--- Score

136. How practical is a particular activity within a process?
<--- Score

137. What level of problem are you experiencing in this topic/Process Area?
<--- Score

138. How long will it take to see substantive process change?
<--- Score

Add up total points for this section:
_____ = Total points for this section

Divided by: _____ (number of statements answered) = _____

Average score for this section

Transfer your score to the CMMI Index at the beginning of the Self-Assessment.

CRITERION #5: IMPROVE:

INTENT: Develop a practical solution. Innovate, establish and test the solution and to measure the results.

In my belief, the answer to this question is clearly defined:

5 Strongly Agree

4 Agree

3 Neutral

2 Disagree

1 Strongly Disagree

1. Should the evaluation be quarterly in sync with the CMMI reporting cycle, annually or a different period?
<--- Score

2. How are the maturity of an agile software development approach and the use of software quality metrics related?
<--- Score

3. Are requirements understandable?
<--- Score

4. How many project staff members involved in the development effort, for each phase and how long?
<--- Score

5. What is the proposed solution and approach to solving the business need or problem?
<--- Score

6. Who decided and how did your organization decide to ascertain your current CMMI maturity level?
<--- Score

7. You only develop software -does adopting the CMM make sense?
<--- Score

8. What tools were used to evaluate the potential solutions?
<--- Score

9. Are there any constraints (technical, political, cultural, or otherwise) that would inhibit certain solutions?
<--- Score

10. Have necessary supporting tools been developed or acquired?
<--- Score

11. Was a pilot designed for the proposed solution(s)?
<--- Score

12. Does your organization (team) have a formal, documented software quality assurance program?
<--- Score

13. Will all the pilots be conducted in parallel or will it be a phased approach?
<--- Score

14. What is the implementation plan?
<--- Score

15. How do you identify risks according to agile principles?
<--- Score

16. How did the team generate the list of possible solutions?
<--- Score

17. How does the solution remove the key sources of issues discovered in the analyze phase?
<--- Score

18. Does SaaS development emphasize different kind of targeted quality (level, characteristics) to traditional software development?
<--- Score

19. Do you know what you have to do to approve/baseline/finalize your documents, designs and code?
<--- Score

20. What is CMMI's impact on utilizing the best solution(s)?

<--- Score

21. What are you improving?
<--- Score

22. How do you change a requirements document?
<--- Score

23. Do you understand variation?
<--- Score

24. What level of risk can the providers take on?
<--- Score

25. Is moving offshore the solution to higher quality software?
<--- Score

26. What are the best practices for software quality assurance when using agile development methodologies?
<--- Score

27. Have the functionality and quality attributes of the system been thoroughly evaluated through sufficient use?
<--- Score

28. Does your organization have a documented procedure for implementing Software Quality Assurance?
<--- Score

29. How is this information used to improve provider performance?
<--- Score

30. How are decisions made?
<--- Score

31. How can you use the CMMI tool to measure and improve your current performance?
<--- Score

32. What error proofing will be done to address some of the discrepancies observed in the 'as is' process?
<--- Score

33. How do you optimize team readiness?
<--- Score

34. If you have already invested in CMMI or OPM3, will you lose the benefit of your investment if you decide to apply the other maturity model as well?
<--- Score

35. Do you know your organizations product delivery and improvement goals and what you must do to support them?
<--- Score

36. What do you need to improve?
<--- Score

37. Is pilot data collected and analyzed?
<--- Score

38. Does the software Quality Assurance function have a management reporting channel separate from the software development project management?
<--- Score

39. Given the fact the agile exists to improve the products you build, and CMMI exists to improve how that work is accomplished, are you using them together?
<--- Score

40. Usability and CMMI: does a higher maturity level in product development mean better usability?
<--- Score

41. Do you know how to store and find records of reviews, inspections, key decisions, etc.?
<--- Score

42. What does it mean to develop a quality software system?
<--- Score

43. What is your risk appetite?
<--- Score

44. What do you do about developer motivation?
<--- Score

45. Do you define the top-level strategy for development of the product?
<--- Score

46. What were the underlying assumptions on the cost-benefit analysis?
<--- Score

47. Is there an Initial Understanding of Requirements secured with all the stakeholders?

<--- Score

48. Does the discipline of CMMI assist the development and maintenance of your training program?
<--- Score

49. How does a CMMI appraisal affect software developers?
<--- Score

50. Is the optimal solution selected based on testing and analysis?
<--- Score

51. What are the mechanisms and methods for evaluating software development tool quality?
<--- Score

52. What is the team's contingency plan for potential problems occurring in implementation?
<--- Score

53. Is a formal system development life-cycle (SDLC) methodology followed?
<--- Score

54. What quality metrics are used by your partners during the software development?
<--- Score

55. Are new and improved process ('should be') maps developed?
<--- Score

56. What is the relation between usage and the

potential improvement of the productivity or quality of the software that is developed?
<--- Score

57. Is there a small-scale pilot for proposed improvement(s)? What conclusions were drawn from the outcomes of a pilot?
<--- Score

58. Are possible solutions generated and tested?
<--- Score

59. What communications are necessary to support the implementation of the solution?
<--- Score

60. Which tools does your organization use for requirements development?
<--- Score

61. Were any criteria developed to assist the team in testing and evaluating potential solutions?
<--- Score

62. How will the team or the process owner(s) monitor the implementation plan to see that it is working as intended?
<--- Score

63. Do you believe that taking on of agile methodologies rather than Heavyweight methodologies have any effect on Software Quality for different levels of development?
<--- Score

**64. Why is CMMI appraisal important for software

development companies?
<--- Score

65. Why use CMMI to visualize improvement?
<--- Score

66. Is a solution implementation plan established, including schedule/work breakdown structure, resources, risk management plan, cost/budget, and control plan?
<--- Score

67. How many project staff members are involved in the development effort, for each phase and how long?
<--- Score

68. Will your organization be subjected to excessive risk?
<--- Score

69. What does the 'should be' process map/design look like?
<--- Score

70. Is the level of service quality improving?
<--- Score

71. Is scrum more effective than the improvement CMMI offers in some way?
<--- Score

72. Which changes will improve the daily work in quality and/or efficiency?
<--- Score

73. Do faster releases improve software quality?
<--- Score

74. What happens when a developer needs to determine which test found a particular bug in code that addresses a specific requirement?
<--- Score

75. Why do other organizations decide not to adopt CMMI?
<--- Score

76. How will the group know that the solution worked?
<--- Score

77. Is a contingency plan established?
<--- Score

78. What opportunities open up as a result of this strategy?
<--- Score

79. What tools were most useful during the improve phase?
<--- Score

80. Repeatability: can the measurement be repeated, given the same definition, to get the same results?
<--- Score

81. Are risk constant through out the project ?
<--- Score

82. Is there a cost/benefit analysis of optimal

solution(s)?
<--- Score

83. What lessons, if any, from a pilot were incorporated into the design of the full-scale solution?
<--- Score

84. Does distributed development affect software quality?
<--- Score

85. How can iec 1131-3 improve the quality of industrial control software?
<--- Score

86. How to optimize team readiness?
<--- Score

87. What tools were used to tap into the creativity and encourage 'outside the box' thinking?
<--- Score

88. What are the mechanisms and methods for evaluating software development tool quality your organization uses?
<--- Score

89. Is there a mapping of CMMI and lean available?
<--- Score

90. Was the system developed at the vendors site?
<--- Score

91. What are the key tasks/best practices to be followed during SDLC to improve software quality?

<--- Score

92. Are the best solutions selected?
<--- Score

93. Do you select the development models to address the activities in the phases?
<--- Score

94. How will you transition to the long-term scope of the improvement effort?
<--- Score

95. What attendant changes will need to be made to ensure that the solution is successful?
<--- Score

96. If the measurement effort is part of a larger improvement effort, what are the expected dependencies between the already stated efforts and this one?
<--- Score

97. Why do (perhaps most) software-developing organizations not use CMMI?
<--- Score

98. What are the key risks faced by your organization in adopting CMMI?
<--- Score

99. Describe the design of the pilot and what tests were conducted, if any?
<--- Score

100. Of what quality is any documentation for the

software?
<--- Score

101. Is the implementation plan designed?
<--- Score

102. Determining when a test has failed might be straightforward, and what information should the tester provide to the developer to help fix the bug this test has discovered?
<--- Score

103. After examining the metrics, what differences in software quality conception held by the team leaders may be concluded from the results?
<--- Score

104. Is CMMI a noteworthy improvement compared to other models and approaches that you have used?
<--- Score

105. Does the software quality assurance (sqa) function have a management reporting channel separate from the software development project management?
<--- Score

106. Where do you need to improve?
<--- Score

107. How does the quality of each component contribute to the quality of the developed software?
<--- Score

108. Are improved process ('should be') maps modified based on pilot data and analysis? <--- Score

Add up total points for this section:
_____ = Total points for this section

Divided by: _____ (number of statements answered) = _____
Average score for this section

Transfer your score to the CMMI Index at the beginning of the Self-Assessment.

CRITERION #6: CONTROL:

INTENT: Implement the practical solution. Maintain the performance and correct possible complications.

In my belief, the answer to this question is clearly defined:

5 Strongly Agree

4 Agree

3 Neutral

2 Disagree

1 Strongly Disagree

1. How do you ensure that your project plan is available for others to see?
<--- Score

2. Has a policy been established to define how to plan & perform the process?
<--- Score

3. Is there a documented and implemented

monitoring plan?
<--- Score

4. Are suggested corrective/restorative actions indicated on the response plan for known causes to problems that might surface?
<--- Score

5. How you monitor the quality of your service?
<--- Score

6. What has machine learning contributed to software quality and what can you expect?
<--- Score

7. Is a response plan established and deployed?
<--- Score

8. What key inputs and outputs are being measured on an ongoing basis?
<--- Score

9. Are there any lessons learned which might help in the project management of CMMI ?
<--- Score

10. Does the CMMI performance meet the customer's requirements?
<--- Score

11. Is reporting being used or needed?
<--- Score

12. Are operating procedures consistent?
<--- Score

13. How much is planned for achieving good quality?
<--- Score

14. How will input, process, and output variables be checked to detect for sub-optimal conditions?
<--- Score

15. Is automated technology used to capture calls for quality monitoring?
<--- Score

16. Is there a transfer of ownership and knowledge to process owner and process team tasked with the responsibilities.
<--- Score

17. Is knowledge gained on process shared and institutionalized?
<--- Score

18. How will the process owner and team be able to hold the gains?
<--- Score

19. Is there a control plan in place for sustaining improvements (short and long-term)?
<--- Score

20. In many organizations the ISO and CMMI based quality efforts are on parallel tracks. what are the plans to move CMMI in line with ISO?
<--- Score

21. What about existing software that maintained in some other version control system?

<--- Score

22. Does your plan consider quality assurance at early phases of the software lifecycle?
<--- Score

23. How do the audits cover planning activities?
<--- Score

24. How is a project management plan document normally organized ?
<--- Score

25. To compare with plans - are you on track or in trouble?
<--- Score

26. Does job training on the documented procedures need to be part of the process team's education and training?
<--- Score

27. How can the Project Planning process area of the CMMI make the sprint planning more robust?
<--- Score

28. Do you have controls in place to ensure that standards of quality are being met for all software development?
<--- Score

29. Is there documentation that will support the successful operation of the improvement?
<--- Score

30. Is there a written organizational policy for

planning and performing measurement activities?
<--- Score

31. Do units that perform similar activities use standard or similar processes?
<--- Score

32. What is the best CMMI transition plan?
<--- Score

33. Have new or revised work instructions resulted?
<--- Score

34. How will the day-to-day responsibilities for monitoring and continual improvement be transferred from the improvement team to the process owner?
<--- Score

35. Are there documented procedures?
<--- Score

36. What factors influence the adoption and spread of model enhancements?
<--- Score

37. How can you strengthen Scrum so that it can scale?
<--- Score

38. How essential are following practices on a project level in large scale agile development?
<--- Score

39. Have you noticed any changes in quality monitoring and improvement systems in the last

year?
<--- Score

40. What other areas of the group might benefit from the CMMI team's improvements, knowledge, and learning?
<--- Score

41. **Do you inspect or plan for quality?**
<--- Score

42. **What are the SEIs plans to move CMMI in line with ISO?**
<--- Score

43. **Which process standards is your organization interested in adopting?**
<--- Score

44. **In an outsourcing environment, can software quality be improved and vendor lock-in avoided by standardizing system documentation?**
<--- Score

45. **Is a cost effective service being demonstrated through accurate capacity planning?**
<--- Score

46. **Do you use any Software Capability Quality standards?**
<--- Score

47. What is the control/monitoring plan?
<--- Score

48. **Can you attend this in your individual capacity**

to learn about applications of processes quality principles in embedded software in automotive industry?

<--- Score

49. How will the process owner verify improvement in present and future sigma levels, process capabilities?

<--- Score

50. How much planning is enough?

<--- Score

51. Has the improved process and its steps been standardized?

<--- Score

52. How will new or emerging customer needs/requirements be checked/communicated to orient the process toward meeting the new specifications and continually reducing variation?

<--- Score

53. How might the group capture best practices and lessons learned so as to leverage improvements?

<--- Score

54. Which international standards and which of requirements should be taken into account for the development of a medical device software quality assurance framework?

<--- Score

55. Is a response plan in place for when the input, process, or output measures indicate an 'out-of-control' condition?

<--- Score

56. What other systems, operations, processes, and infrastructures (hiring practices, staffing, training, incentives/rewards, metrics/dashboards/scorecards, etc.) need updates, additions, changes, or deletions in order to facilitate knowledge transfer and improvements?
<--- Score

57. Can standardizing system documentation lead to better software quality and lower risk of vendor lock-in?
<--- Score

58. What are the induction processes a project manager must plan for team members?
<--- Score

59. You need to conduct a retrospective meeting prior to planning the next sprint. Do you know what you should do?
<--- Score

60. Is it possible to develop an effective and efficient process architecture that is based on multiple standards?
<--- Score

61. What lessons learned from past failures and successes could be beneficial in preparation for this effort?
<--- Score

62. What are the critical parameters to watch?
<--- Score

63. What quality tools were useful in the control phase?
<--- Score

64. What is the recommended frequency of auditing?
<--- Score

65. Who is the CMMI process owner?
<--- Score

66. What are your expectations with regard to your planning and preparation prior to your CMMI SCAMPI Class B Appraisal?
<--- Score

67. Does the response plan contain a definite closed loop continual improvement scheme (e.g., plan-do-check-act)?
<--- Score

68. Is new knowledge gained imbedded in the response plan?
<--- Score

69. What factors would prevent the widespread adoption of CMMI?
<--- Score

70. Strategic planning or an agile environment: are they mutually exclusive?
<--- Score

71. Is there a standardized process?
<--- Score

72. Do you plan to replace any infrastructure with

cloud solutions in the upcoming fiscal year?
<--- Score

73. What are your expectations with regard to your planning and preparation prior to your CMMI SCAMPI Class A Appraisal?
<--- Score

74. Does a troubleshooting guide exist or is it needed?
<--- Score

75. Does your organization have experience with developing and following a process, and can it support the development of common, standard processes?
<--- Score

76. What obstacles or challenges do you face as you try to gain widespread acceptance of business process efforts at your organization?
<--- Score

77. How would potential learning curves affect the performance of the proposed process changes?
<--- Score

78. What have you learned and how have you modified your implementation process over time?
<--- Score

79. Are new process steps, standards, and documentation ingrained into normal operations?
<--- Score

80. What other activities (project planning, project management, customer status reviews, process

improvement, etc.) will benefit from measurement results?
<--- Score

81. Has a plan been defined and documented for performing the process?
<--- Score

82. Does your organization have a standard, enterprise-wide business process methodology?
<--- Score

83. Are standard process models defined for each major process?
<--- Score

84. Is the enterprise architecture plan adhered to?
<--- Score

85. What should the next improvement project be that is related to CMMI?
<--- Score

86. Are all safe practices reflected in the proposed safe maturity model?
<--- Score

87. How will report readings be checked to effectively monitor performance?
<--- Score

88. Is there a recommended audit plan for routine surveillance inspections of CMMI's gains?
<--- Score

89. Who should be involved in the improvement

strategy, plan, creation and implementation?
<--- Score

90. How do you verify that the requirements are correct and that they reflect what the users want?
<--- Score

91. How did the process maturity framework spread?
<--- Score

92. Does your organization have standard process models for each of its value chains?
<--- Score

93. Will any special training be provided for results interpretation?
<--- Score

94. Are documented procedures clear and easy to follow for the operators?
<--- Score

95. What are the benefits and challenges of adopting Scaled Agile Framework in your organization?
<--- Score

Add up total points for this section:
_____ = Total points for this section

Divided by: _____ (number of statements answered) = _____
Average score for this section

Transfer your score to the CMMI Index at

the beginning of the Self-Assessment.

CRITERION #7: SUSTAIN:

INTENT: Retain the benefits.

In my belief, the answer to this question is clearly defined:

5 Strongly Agree

4 Agree

3 Neutral

2 Disagree

1 Strongly Disagree

1. Is there a limit to growth?
<--- Score

2. Has a regulator ever asked about using a maturity model or considered using a maturity model?
<--- Score

3. Customer - who is it being performed for?
<--- Score

4. Do you feel crushed by a rigid, one size fits all view of the CMMI?
<--- Score

5. How do you get high performance from high maturity?
<--- Score

6. What specifically does the system that will be designed have to do?
<--- Score

7. What quality incentives and metrics should be used?
<--- Score

8. Is spending in IT projects constant through out the project?
<--- Score

9. DevOps is fundamentally about culture and about the quality of your application. And by quality the specific software engineering term of quality is meant, of different quality attributes. What matters to you?
<--- Score

10. What are the the benefits of using CMMI?
<--- Score

11. Is there a way that you can harness the power of CMMI and SCAMPI to address Information Security?
<--- Score

12. Are the activities performed for software

quality management reviewed with senior management on a periodic basis?
<--- Score

13. What method do you recommend?
<--- Score

14. If 90% of the projects tests passed today, is that good?
<--- Score

15. What products do the activities of the assessment method deliver?
<--- Score

16. Do you provide configuration or other logistics services to others?
<--- Score

17. Do software quality assurance test programs undergo the same production cycle and method (except q/a) as the software they test?
<--- Score

18. What is the relationship between the CMMI and the other CMM-based models?
<--- Score

19. Where can you view CMMI appraisal ratings?
<--- Score

20. What are the objectives of software quality assurance?
<--- Score

21. Competing in the Software Industry-Will CMMI

Certification Help?
<--- Score

22. Are there primary studies related with the combined use of agile practices and CMMI?
<--- Score

23. How you review client satisfaction?
<--- Score

24. Can services be recovered from disasters or major disruptions within agreed timeframes?
<--- Score

25. What motivated CMM?
<--- Score

26. Who will facilitate the team and process?
<--- Score

27. Are you really that bad?
<--- Score

28. Is the service as reliable as agreed?
<--- Score

29. How would the ITS project owner use CMMI for contracting purposes?
<--- Score

30. How can CMM help?
<--- Score

31. CMMI implementation: does it really benefit project teams?
<--- Score

32. Are the risks fully understood, reasonable and manageable?
<--- Score

33. What features should be demoted for later release?
<--- Score

34. Do you have any obstacles?
<--- Score

35. What if you fail?
<--- Score

36. Is appropriate, agreed service availability being provided?
<--- Score

37. Where is CMMI being used effectively?
<--- Score

38. Is there any way to speed up the process?
<--- Score

39. How do you get authorized with CMMI-SVC?
<--- Score

40. How do you assess adequate quality in your software products?
<--- Score

41. Is your CMMI implementation being done in the leanest way possible?
<--- Score

42. Are you aware of any common metrics associated with your industry for maturity?
<--- Score

43. Is the project management office a component of the portfolio management office?
<--- Score

44. Is this compatible with an engineering design practice serving both functional and safety goals?
<--- Score

45. Lean six sigma, CMMI, and agile methods: can they co-exist?
<--- Score

46. What are the tools for software quality?
<--- Score

47. What is the relationship between PSM and CMMI?
<--- Score

48. How long is your sw-CMM certification good for?
<--- Score

49. Do you avoid imprecise statements like, the system shall be easy to use?
<--- Score

50. Is there support for the validity of quality metrics or outcomes used in the model?
<--- Score

51. Can your iso auditor use the work of others

involved in appraisals based on CMMI-dev?
<--- Score

52. Is it worth it?
<--- Score

53. What types of services does CMMI-svc cover?
<--- Score

54. What else could be done to facilitate your adoption of CMMI?
<--- Score

55. What is the difference between Software Testing and Software Quality Assurance?
<--- Score

56. Why do you want to do it?
<--- Score

57. When would you expect to achieve the business goals from adopting CMMI?
<--- Score

58. How do you know what evidence to gather?
<--- Score

59. What steps are taken for quality assurance of any release of the software?
<--- Score

60. Has your organization communicated your maturity assessment with regulators?
<--- Score

61. How does your organization assure the

quality and security of publicly available software modules and libraries used within your products?
<--- Score

62. What are the types of projects that are being considered for the Project Management Office (PMO)?
<--- Score

63. Management structure - who leads what work?
<--- Score

64. What features fit within the deadline?
<--- Score

65. What are the processes for audit reporting and management?
<--- Score

66. What alternative responses are available to manage risk?
<--- Score

67. How do you know what the objectives and expected outcomes should be for Maintenance?
<--- Score

68. How do you set benchmarks ?
<--- Score

69. What are quality criteria for how software projects are run and managed?
<--- Score

70. Representations: continuous or staged?
<--- Score

71. Relevant stakeholders are included to address questions as : Is the new functionality operating effectively?
<--- Score

72. How can you use CMMI with agile principles?
<--- Score

73. How do you track the technical activities in your project?
<--- Score

74. What statistical confidence level are you using to predict the faults?
<--- Score

75. Why CMMI?
<--- Score

76. What keeps you up at night?
<--- Score

77. Are the agile levels of the proposed SAFe Maturity Model comprehensive enough?
<--- Score

78. What if success with agile or CMMI really has nothing to do with agile or CMMI?
<--- Score

79. How to derive the architecture using Quality Attributes?
<--- Score

**80. What other consulting or independent

contractor services have you rendered?
<--- Score

81. Did your provider seem to have access to your electronic medical record?
<--- Score

82. In addition to years in the industry, innovation is also an essential quality of a software vendor. Does your vendor have a proven track record of industry innovation?
<--- Score

83. Now that carnegie-mellon owns, operates and supports, what do you think the future is for CMMI?
<--- Score

84. How will you use this maturity model for self-assessment in the future and why or why not?
<--- Score

85. What are the underlying principles of CMMI as they relate to productivity, predictability, and speed?
<--- Score

86. What CMMI process areas are addressed?
<--- Score

87. Is there a GUI, a command line or some other type of interface?
<--- Score

88. What are the external characteristics of good quality software?

<--- Score

89. What deliverables and communications may you expect from you at the conclusion of your CMMI SCAMPI Class A Appraisal?
<--- Score

90. How could this Maturity Model be helpful to determine the status of maturity in your organization?
<--- Score

91. Is the quality information for network providers or all providers?
<--- Score

92. Do you describe the functionality of the system in the language of the customer?
<--- Score

93. What test maturity models have researchers and practitioners proposed?
<--- Score

94. How does your organization stack up to the industry in software quality and testing?
<--- Score

95. Which changes will negatively affect your work in quality and/or efficiency?
<--- Score

96. Why do only the software engineers get to do CMMI?
<--- Score

97. Are software quality assurance tests a part of the general hardware acceptance test on the customers machine before it leaves the factory?
<--- Score

98. Is your product quality what you expect it to be?
<--- Score

99. Do you use a sub-contractor for subrogation collections?
<--- Score

100. Has your organization communicated your Maturity Model assessment with regulators?
<--- Score

101. How does software engineering encourage software quality through broader education at all levels of your organization?
<--- Score

102. Why are you doing this?
<--- Score

103. What should be included in each appraisal?
<--- Score

104. How are your operations impacted with the implementation of CMMI-SVC?
<--- Score

105. When and why to use CMMI-SVC?
<--- Score

106. What are the benefits to your organization for

moving up the CMMI-ACQ maturity levels?
<--- Score

107. What is your rate of defects?
<--- Score

108. What should be the main added value of using a Continuous Delivery Maturity Model?
<--- Score

109. What is being done in the name of CMMI that is not necessary?
<--- Score

110. Is it possible to integrate CMMI and agile practices like Scrum to achieve the benefits from both - or even more?
<--- Score

111. What is included in the CMM?
<--- Score

112. Have you and your organization used any tools to benchmark the maturity model?
<--- Score

113. Can you do it?
<--- Score

114. How do you estimate maintenance project and change requests?
<--- Score

115. How can you leverage your organizations quality strategy?
<--- Score

116. Are you certified by the Software Engineering Institute (SEI) to conduct CMMI SCAMPI appraisals as a Lead Appraiser?
<--- Score

117. Aligning CMMI & itil where are you and which way do you go?
<--- Score

118. Before writing any code, do the people responsible for building a new application start by thinking about its structure? What parts should the application have?
<--- Score

119. What is the level of IT innovation that occurs within your organization?
<--- Score

120. Does your organization implementing CMMI target the achievement of a particular CMMI maturity level?
<--- Score

121. What is the baseline level of competency?
<--- Score

122. How do you leverage the investment when moving to CMMI?
<--- Score

123. How can CMMI help?
<--- Score

124. CMMI and agile: can they co-exist?

<--- Score

125. What is the key limitation for government in approaching CMMI?
<--- Score

126. What particular web technologies should the contractor be prepared to support?
<--- Score

127. Why you should do business with your organization that is appraised for CMMI?
<--- Score

128. Does the CMMI framework address unique software maintenance aspects?
<--- Score

129. Has your organization been able to realize your strategic goals implementing maturity models?
<--- Score

130. What goal are you trying to achieve?
<--- Score

131. What is the sequence of uml diagrams in the project?
<--- Score

132. How long does it take?
<--- Score

133. Who benefits from CMMI today?
<--- Score

134. How must the project manager react under pressured projects?
<--- Score

135. Does your CMMI include or exclude small projects?
<--- Score

136. How might you adapt or augment the CMMI material to address Financial Management?
<--- Score

137. What is your software quality assurance?
<--- Score

138. Has software management and quality assurance been used for tool software?
<--- Score

139. What is the basis for the CMMI-SVC model?
<--- Score

140. Which element is maturing?
<--- Score

141. To what extent does dispersion in software tasks affect software productivity and quality?
<--- Score

142. How can agile & CMMI work together to help produce better software?
<--- Score

143. Should you implement CMMI-DEV independently of ISO 9001, or are there some areas where they overlap?

<--- Score

144. Should you have an appraisal?
<--- Score

145. Are you scrumming too much?
<--- Score

146. Why adopt CMM?
<--- Score

147. In what extent it is possible to combine CMMI and PMBOK with the agile manifesto?
<--- Score

148. Does your organization have a Software Quality Assurance you Team?
<--- Score

149. Does the software adequately meet its quality factors?
<--- Score

150. What do you get when a vendor has a CMMI rating?
<--- Score

151. What strategy should lead you?
<--- Score

152. Are you building it right?
<--- Score

153. Why the discord between Agile and CMMI camps?
<--- Score

154. Do software quality assurance test programs undergo the same production cycle and method (except QA) as the software they test?
<--- Score

155. Which maturity model has your organization used?
<--- Score

156. How can you get the word out about your meetings and activities?
<--- Score

157. What constitutes a maturity model for project-based management?
<--- Score

158. What are your business goals?
<--- Score

159. What if your organization does want to leverage CMMI?
<--- Score

160. Are the symptoms of level one present?
<--- Score

161. What do you expect to achieve if you invest time and money in using a particular maturity model to move your organization forward?
<--- Score

162. Have stakeholders been negatively affected?
<--- Score

163. How will it be sustained?
<--- Score

164. Is CMMI adequate for guiding process improvement?
<--- Score

165. Why do people believe the CMM has little value?
<--- Score

166. What is the quality of technical support for the application software?
<--- Score

167. Is it worth doing?
<--- Score

168. Agile and CMMI where do they run into problems?
<--- Score

169. What does sunsetting the sw-CMM mean?
<--- Score

170. How will the system interact with its users. Is there a GUI, a command line or some other type of interface?
<--- Score

171. Why outsource application support?
<--- Score

172. What is the value of CMMI level 5?
<--- Score

173. Where can it be used?
<--- Score

174. Could any agile practice be used in combination with CMMI?
<--- Score

175. To what level will you apply the CMMI Framework in your organization?
<--- Score

176. How do you start with agile CMMI?
<--- Score

177. How do you practically implement form based authentication?
<--- Score

178. Key messages - while they will change over time, what are the three core messages that carry forward through all of your initiatives?
<--- Score

179. What is the benefit of using the CMMI?
<--- Score

180. Are there enough resources (or too many) to meet demand for services?
<--- Score

181. What does it mean to be appraised as CMMI-dev level 3?
<--- Score

182. What does it take to enhance the quantity and quality of corresponding evidence?

<--- Score

183. Which projects (new, existing) are expected to participate?
<--- Score

184. Combining agile with CMMI, is it working?
<--- Score

185. Can both, CMMI and agile methods, mutually benefit from each other?
<--- Score

186. What systems/processes must you excel at?
<--- Score

187. Does your CMMI statement of work include or exclude small projects?
<--- Score

188. What deliverables and communications may you expect from you at the conclusion of your CMMI SCAMPI Class B Appraisal?
<--- Score

189. Do you establish and maintain the budget and schedule including: resources and facilities, time phasing of activities and schedule activities?
<--- Score

190. How would you best describe your familiarity with CMMI?
<--- Score

191. What is included in the CMMI?
<--- Score

192. How will you accomplish this?
<--- Score

193. Will you be doing reviews?
<--- Score

194. How do you determine whether the current sprint should be canceled. Under what circumstances should you cancel the current sprint?
<--- Score

195. Who is included in the target audience?
<--- Score

196. What sprint backlog item are you working on?
<--- Score

197. Is spending in IT projects constant throughout the project?
<--- Score

198. What do you know about human rights in relation to your products and services?
<--- Score

199. Has configuration management and quality assurance been used for tool software?
<--- Score

200. What attributes should a software system have in order to be of high quality?
<--- Score

201. How do you report the status of your project?

<--- Score

202. What is the quality of the software?
<--- Score

203. What evidence is sufficient to satisfy the practice?
<--- Score

204. What are your expectations with regard to the expected duration of your CMMI SCAMPI Class A Appraisal?
<--- Score

205. How long has your organization been implementing maturity models?
<--- Score

206. How many personnel should the contractor anticipate it will have to train?
<--- Score

207. How are team members kept informed about the current status of the project?
<--- Score

208. Are the key business and technology risks being managed?
<--- Score

209. Are you getting more business moving to a higher maturity?
<--- Score

210. Do you establish quality assurance reports?
<--- Score

211. Do you have any quality assurance activities for software projects?
<--- Score

212. Is there any influence from the teams size in the agile practices use with CMMI culture?
<--- Score

213. How many years of experience do you have with Agile?
<--- Score

214. What presumptions have been made about resource availability, management commitment, practitioner buy-in etc.?
<--- Score

215. Does it work in practice?
<--- Score

216. What is the industrys experience with the CMM?
<--- Score

217. Does management have the right priorities among projects?
<--- Score

218. What could you do better?
<--- Score

219. Are risk management tasks balanced centrally and locally?
<--- Score

220. Can your scampi lead appraiser use the work of others involved in ISO audits?
<--- Score

221. What is the return on investment?
<--- Score

222. Are you producing high-quality and reliable software?
<--- Score

223. When must it be addressed?
<--- Score

224. Is CMMI useful and usable in small settings?
<--- Score

225. What system, practice, and person-level factors are associated with the model outcomes?
<--- Score

226. How do you manage conflict in the project team?
<--- Score

227. Could you include coverage of information security in a SCAMPI appraisal that covered CMMI-SVC as well?
<--- Score

228. How well do you know your suppliers?
<--- Score

229. Are your expectations realistic?
<--- Score

230. Who are the stakeholders?
<--- Score

231. If you are going to be CMMI compliant, do you take an agile approach or better yet, a disciplined agile approach when doing so?
<--- Score

232. Is a team code review invalid if a single team member is missing?
<--- Score

233. Can a manufacturing quality model work for software?
<--- Score

234. What if any CMMI training have you received?
<--- Score

235. What are your expectations with regard to your participation and involvement during your CMMI SCAMPI Class A Appraisal?
<--- Score

236. When working on your next maturity level - when to transition or wait?
<--- Score

237. What if the application is changing frequently?
<--- Score

238. How do you turn the CMMI-x into SOIs and SOPs?
<--- Score

239. What according to you is a quality software product?
<--- Score

240. How would you describe the strategies you use for managing software quality?
<--- Score

241. Are there are any other tools your organization uses to assess maturity?
<--- Score

242. How has six sigma been used in your software projects?
<--- Score

243. If you do have ISO 20000, how much CMMI-SVC do you get?
<--- Score

244. Competing in the Software Industry-Will CMM Certification Help?
<--- Score

245. Do you know what skills you should have?
<--- Score

246. What are all the skills you will be looking at if you have to hire a project manager?
<--- Score

247. Which features are most critical?
<--- Score

248. How do you track the size or changes to size of the work products in your project?

<--- Score

249. If you are doing Scrum, does this automatically give you a CMMI ML3?
<--- Score

250. What is quality software?
<--- Score

251. How does CMMI partner with itil?
<--- Score

252. Has there been any change in your organizations ratings in the last two years?
<--- Score

253. What properties make a software system of high quality?
<--- Score

254. What are the challenges associated with generic and medical device software quality assurance?
<--- Score

255. Why are agile practices implemented in organizations with CMMI culture?
<--- Score

256. Why CMMI level 3?
<--- Score

257. What can you expect?
<--- Score

258. Are service level agreements tracked?

<--- Score

259. What services are covered?
<--- Score

260. What are the goals of software quality assurance?
<--- Score

261. What is the advantage of implementing CMMI in your organization?
<--- Score

262. How did you choose the appropriate lifecycle for your project?
<--- Score

263. Can the customer just call up and ask for something new?
<--- Score

264. What are your main reasons / motivations for adopting CMMI?
<--- Score

265. What are your expectations with regard to the expected duration of your CMMI SCAMPI Class B Appraisal?
<--- Score

266. What is the defining quality of a good software system, and what are its main characteristics?
<--- Score

267. What is the relationship between CMMI-SVC

and ITIL?
<--- Score

268. What are your expectations with regard to your participation and involvement during your CMMI SCAMPI Class B Appraisal?
<--- Score

269. Is there really a positive correlation between business success and high maturity levels?
<--- Score

270. Can psp/tsp methods be applied to the ERP implementation?
<--- Score

271. How does the CMM treat maintenance?
<--- Score

272. How can you apply Lean techniques to CMMI models?
<--- Score

273. Who manages supplier risk management in your organization?
<--- Score

274. Why is this important?
<--- Score

275. What are the principal activities of a modern quality system?
<--- Score

276. Do you have the optimal project management team structure?

<--- Score

277. Has your organization used any tools to benchmark your maturity model?
<--- Score

278. What does product quality really mean?
<--- Score

279. Does CMMI bring anything of value to the table for agile teams?
<--- Score

280. Are you involved in any of the individual organization level implementation practices?
<--- Score

281. What is the difference between the different CMMI Levels?
<--- Score

282. How efficient is your quality performance?
<--- Score

283. What is your vision of CMMI beyond version 1.3?
<--- Score

284. What assumptions are made about the solution and approach?
<--- Score

285. Is your team clear on how to interact with project stakeholders?
<--- Score

286. Assess the security and integrity of system and application software. Does your organization have adequate quality assurance and testing programs?
<--- Score

287. Does the CMM framework address unique software maintenance aspects?
<--- Score

288. Scrum and CMMI - does it fit together?
<--- Score

289. What strategies do you use that are most effective for managing software quality?
<--- Score

290. What is the benefit of combining Scrum and CMMI?
<--- Score

291. How well are you doing it?
<--- Score

292. How well qualified is the individual, team, or organization to conduct the proposed activities?
<--- Score

293. Are you certified by the SEI to conduct CMMI SCAMPI Class A and B Appraisals?
<--- Score

294. What do you do if your organization wants to do a CMMI-SVC appraisal?
<--- Score

295. How effective is your IT Governance?
<--- Score

296. What is the relationship between software quality and software maintenance?
<--- Score

297. What are the advantages/disadvantages in adopting the CMM for you?
<--- Score

298. What is the real structure that gets things done?
<--- Score

299. What is the key limitation for your organization in approaching CMMI?
<--- Score

300. What can you promise within a Service Level Agreement to the end customer?
<--- Score

301. What is your organizations software quality assurance?
<--- Score

302. Enterprise architecture: have you answered the who, what, where, when, why, how?
<--- Score

303. Can you account for staged and continuous models in CMMI?
<--- Score

304. What are your goals, purposes and

expectations for a particular task?
<--- Score

305. Can you integrate quality management and risk management?
<--- Score

306. What is your experience in the usage of Continuous Delivery Maturity Models?
<--- Score

307. What is the capability maturity model (CMM)?
<--- Score

308. While frequent builds are useful, running a build for each checked-in code change is the cornerstone of continuous integration, what happens if a change breaks the build?
<--- Score

309. What will you have done by tomorrows Scrum?
<--- Score

310. Why did you prefer Scrum?
<--- Score

311. Would you consider implementing an energy management maturity model in your organization?
<--- Score

312. Does SAP provide any restrictions which do not allow the highest maturity levels to be reached?
<--- Score

313. Does your organization have a project and portfolio management software package?
<--- Score

314. Is software used in the Quality Management System validated prior to initial use, and as appropriate, after changes?
<--- Score

315. Are there lessons from corresponding other disciplines that can be used in the CMMI?
<--- Score

316. Are customer expectations and your capabilities aligned?
<--- Score

317. What does it take for your organization to achieve ISO registration or attain a CMMI maturity level?
<--- Score

318. Do you establish reports of quality trends?
<--- Score

319. Where do you see yourself after three years?
<--- Score

320. How many features can be built within a 24-week schedule?
<--- Score

321. How does CMMI complement agile and what benefits can you expect to see?
<--- Score

322. What groups (product lines) are expected to participate?
<--- Score

323. Why was the software quality assurance team leader satisfied with the system?
<--- Score

324. Are training program activities reviewed on a periodic basis?
<--- Score

325. What strategies do you use that are least effective for managing software quality?
<--- Score

326. Do the existing SDLC models support to build Quality features in the software product?
<--- Score

327. What would you do if you found out that a contractor was in a conflict of interest situation?
<--- Score

328. How can you make it better?
<--- Score

329. Has your organization been able to realize strategic goals by implementing a maturity model?
<--- Score

330. When will it happen?
<--- Score

331. How do you get your team working on the same project goal?
<--- Score

332. How do you estimate the effort for your project?
<--- Score

333. Do you review the status and history of quality assurance activities as necessary?
<--- Score

334. Does the system export reports and other information for use by the contractor?
<--- Score

335. When is it ready to ship?
<--- Score

336. Do you build and maintain records of quality assurance activities?
<--- Score

337. Is the quality of the software acceptable?
<--- Score

338. How is CMMI different from other quality system models?
<--- Score

339. Will you meet your next deliverable milestone?
<--- Score

340. Are the projects visibly supported by management?

<--- Score

Add up total points for this section:
_____ = Total points for this section

Divided by: _____ (number of statements answered) = _____
Average score for this section

Transfer your score to the CMMI Index at the beginning of the Self-Assessment.

CMMI and Managing Projects, Criteria for Project Managers:

1.0 Initiating Process Group: CMMI

1. What must be done?

2. What will be the pressing issues of tomorrow?

3. What is the stake of others in your CMMI project?

4. How do you help others satisfy needs?

5. What are the overarching issues of your organization?

6. During which stage of Risk planning are risks prioritized based on probability and impact?

7. First of all, should any action be taken?

8. What is the NEXT thing to do?

9. The process to Manage Stakeholders is part of which process group?

10. Are you just doing busywork to pass the time?

11. Where must it be done?

12. Are stakeholders properly informed about the status of the CMMI project?

13. Did you use a contractor or vendor?

14. Did the CMMI project team have the right skills?

15. Contingency planning. if a risk event occurs, what

will you do?

16. Who does what?

17. Did the CMMI project team have the right skills?

18. How will you know you did it?

19. How well defined and documented were the CMMI project management processes you chose to use?

20. What technical work to do in each phase?

1.1 Project Charter: CMMI

21. What is in it for you?

22. What are some examples of a business case?

23. Major high-level milestone targets: what events measure progress?

24. When is a charter needed?

25. Name and describe the elements that deal with providing the detail?

26. What are the constraints?

27. When do you use a CMMI project Charter?

28. Are you building in-house ?

29. Why the improvements?

30. CMMI project deliverables: what is the CMMI project going to produce?

31. When?

32. Strategic fit: what is the strategic initiative identifier for this CMMI project?

33. Who is the sponsor?

34. What is the justification?

35. For whom?

36. Assumptions and constraints: what assumptions were made in defining the CMMI project?

37. Why is it important?

38. Why do you need to manage scope?

39. Why use a CMMI project charter?

40. What goes into your CMMI project Charter?

1.2 Stakeholder Register: CMMI

41. How big is the gap?

42. What opportunities exist to provide communications?

43. Is your organization ready for change?

44. How should employers make voices heard?

45. How will reports be created?

46. Who is managing stakeholder engagement?

47. What is the power of the stakeholder?

48. What are the major CMMI project milestones requiring communications or providing communications opportunities?

49. What & Why?

50. Who wants to talk about Security?

51. How much influence do they have on the CMMI project?

52. Who are the stakeholders?

1.3 Stakeholder Analysis Matrix: CMMI

53. Partnership opportunities/synergies?

54. Who will promote/support the CMMI project, provided that they are involved?

55. Do the stakeholders goals and expectations support or conflict with the CMMI project goals?

56. Advantages of proposition?

57. What do people from other organizations see as your organizations weaknesses?

58. If you can not fix it, how do you do it differently?

59. Business and product development?

60. Who determines value?

61. How to measure the achievement of the Immediate Objective?

62. Are the required specifications for products or services changing?

63. Who can contribute financial or technical resources towards the work?

64. What is your Risk Management?

65. Gaps in capabilities?

66. Sustainable financial backing?

67. What makes a person a stakeholder?

68. Processes, systems, it, communications?

69. What is the stakeholders mandate, what is mission?

70. What mechanisms are proposed to monitor and measure CMMI project performance in terms of social development outcomes?

71. Cultural, attitudinal, behavioural?

2.0 Planning Process Group: CMMI

72. In what way has the program contributed towards the issue culture and development included on the public agenda?

73. Did the program design/ implementation strategy adequately address the planning stage necessary to set up structures, hire staff etc.?

74. Mitigate. what will you do to minimize the impact should a risk event occur?

75. Is the duration of the program sufficient to ensure a cycle that will CMMI project the sustainability of the interventions?

76. What types of differentiated effects are resulting from the CMMI project and to what extent?

77. To what extent have public/private national resources and/or counterparts been mobilized to contribute to the programs objective and produce results and impacts?

78. CMMI project assessment; why did you do this CMMI project?

79. Do the partners have sufficient financial capacity to keep up the benefits produced by the programme?

80. In what ways can the governance of the CMMI project be improved so that it has greater likelihood of achieving future sustainability?

81. Will the products created live up to the necessary quality?

82. Have operating capacities been created and/or reinforced in partners?

83. What do they need to know about the CMMI project?

84. Why do it CMMI projects fail?

85. Are there efficient coordination mechanisms to avoid overloading the counterparts, participating stakeholders?

86. To what extent and in what ways are the CMMI project contributing to progress towards organizational reform?

87. Is the CMMI project making progress in helping to achieve the set results?

88. If a task is partitionable, is this a sufficient condition to reduce the CMMI project duration?

89. To what extent are the visions and actions of the partners consistent or divergent with regard to the program?

90. Are the necessary foundations in place to ensure the sustainability of the results of the CMMI project?

91. How does activity resource estimation affect activity duration estimation?

2.1 Project Management Plan: CMMI

92. What are the assumptions?

93. If the CMMI project management plan is a comprehensive document that guides you in CMMI project execution and control, then what should it NOT contain?

94. What are the deliverables?

95. Is there anything you would now do differently on your CMMI project based on past experience?

96. How well are you able to manage your risk?

97. What is CMMI project scope management?

98. Did the planning effort collaborate to develop solutions that integrate expertise, policies, programs, and CMMI projects across entities?

99. Are there non-structural buyout or relocation recommendations?

100. How can you best help your organization to develop consistent practices in CMMI project management planning stages?

101. What went right?

102. Is there an incremental analysis/cost effectiveness analysis of proposed mitigation features based on an approved method and using an accepted

model?

103. Is the budget realistic?

104. What are the assigned resources?

105. Does the implementation plan have an appropriate division of responsibilities?

106. What does management expect of PMs?

107. What would you do differently what did not work?

108. Was the peer (technical) review of the cost estimates duly coordinated with the cost estimate center of expertise and addressed in the review documentation and certification?

109. Are the existing and future without-plan conditions reasonable and appropriate?

110. What would you do differently?

2.2 Scope Management Plan: CMMI

111. Has a quality assurance plan been developed for the CMMI project?

112. Have CMMI project team accountabilities & responsibilities been clearly defined?

113. Have all necessary approvals been obtained?

114. Are procurement deliverables arriving on time and to specification?

115. Have the scope, objectives, costs, benefits and impacts been communicated to all involved and/or impacted stakeholders and work groups?

116. Quality standards - are controls in place to ensure that the work was not only completed and also completed to meet specific standards?

117. Does the CMMI project have a Statement of Work?

118. Does a documented CMMI project organizational policy & plan (i.e. governance model) exist?

119. How do you plan to control Scope Creep?

120. Are agendas created for each meeting with meeting objectives, meeting topics, invitee list, and action items from past meetings?

121. What is the need the CMMI project will address?

122. What are the risks of not having good inter-organization cooperation on the CMMI project?

123. What should you drop in order to add something new?

124. Are CMMI project contact logs kept up to date?

125. Describe the process for accepting the CMMI project deliverables. Will the CMMI project deliverables become accepted in writing?

126. Are CMMI project team members involved in detailed estimating and scheduling?

127. Has a structured approach been used to break work effort into manageable components (WBS)?

128. Organizational unit (e.g., department, team, or person) who will accept responsibility for satisfactory completion of the item?

129. How relevant is this attribute to this CMMI project or audit?

130. How many changes are you making?

2.3 Requirements Management Plan: CMMI

131. Is the change control process documented?

132. What cost metrics will be used?

133. Should you include sub-activities?

134. After the requirements are gathered and set forth on the requirements register, theyre little more than a laundry list of items. Some may be duplicates, some might conflict with others and some will be too broad or too vague to understand. Describe how the requirements will be analyzed. Who will perform the analysis?

135. How will you develop the schedule of requirements activities?

136. What is the earliest finish date for this CMMI project if it is scheduled to start on ...?

137. Why manage requirements?

138. The wbs is developed as part of a joint planning session. and how do you know that youhave done this right?

139. How will you communicate scheduled tasks to other team members?

140. Will the CMMI project requirements become

approved in writing?

141. Could inaccurate or incomplete requirements in this CMMI project create a serious risk for the business?

142. Has the requirements team been instructed in the Change Control process?

143. Do you really need to write this document at all?

144. Are actual resource expenditures versus planned still acceptable?

145. To see if a requirement statement is sufficiently well-defined, read it from the developers perspective. Mentally add the phrase, call me when youre done to the end of the requirement and see if that makes you nervous. In other words, would you need additional clarification from the author to understand the requirement well enough to design and implement it?

146. Is stakeholder risk tolerance an important factor for the requirements process in this CMMI project?

147. Controlling CMMI project requirements involves monitoring the status of the CMMI project requirements and managing changes to the requirements. Who is responsible for monitoring and tracking the CMMI project requirements?

148. Is there formal agreement on who has authority to approve a change in requirements?

149. Who will finally present the work or product(s) for acceptance?

2.4 Requirements Documentation: CMMI

150. What facilities must be supported by the system?

151. Who provides requirements?

152. What are the attributes of a customer?

153. Do your constraints stand?

154. What marketing channels do you want to use: e-mail, letter or sms?

155. What are the potential disadvantages/ advantages?

156. Have the benefits identified with the system being identified clearly?

157. Is the requirement properly understood?

158. How do you know when a Requirement is accurate enough?

159. Is the origin of the requirement clearly stated?

160. How to document system requirements?

161. How will the proposed CMMI project help?

162. How do you get the user to tell you what they want?

163. Has requirements gathering uncovered information that would necessitate changes?

164. How does what is being described meet the business need?

165. How can you document system requirements?

166. Where do system and software requirements come from, what are sources?

167. Basic work/business process; high-level, what is being touched?

168. Do technical resources exist?

169. If applicable; are there issues linked with the fact that this is an offshore CMMI project?

2.5 Requirements Traceability Matrix: CMMI

170. Is there a requirements traceability process in place?

171. Why use a WBS?

172. How do you manage scope?

173. What percentage of CMMI projects are producing traceability matrices between requirements and other work products?

174. What are the chronologies, contingencies, consequences, criteria?

175. How will it affect the stakeholders personally in career?

176. How small is small enough?

177. What is the WBS?

178. Do you have a clear understanding of all subcontracts in place?

179. Describe the process for approving requirements so they can be added to the traceability matrix and CMMI project work can be performed. Will the CMMI project requirements become approved in writing?

180. Why do you manage scope?

181. Will you use a Requirements Traceability Matrix?

2.6 Project Scope Statement: CMMI

182. Elements of scope management that deal with concept development ?

183. How often will scope changes be reviewed?

184. Are the input requirements from the team members clearly documented and communicated?

185. Any new risks introduced or old risks impacted. Are there issues that could affect the existing requirements for the result, service, or product if the scope changes?

186. What is change?

187. If there is an independent oversight contractor, have they signed off on the CMMI project Plan?

188. Is there a Change Management Board?

189. Do you anticipate new stakeholders joining the CMMI project over time?

190. Will the risk status be reported to management on a regular and frequent basis?

191. Which risks does the CMMI project focus on?

192. Are there specific processes you will use to evaluate and approve/reject changes?

193. Is the CMMI project sponsor function identified

and defined?

194. Is the plan for CMMI project resources adequate?

195. Will the risk documents be filed?

196. Is your organization structure appropriate for the CMMI projects size and complexity?

197. Did your CMMI project ask for this?

198. Does the scope statement still need some clarity?

199. Will there be a Change Control Process in place?

2.7 Assumption and Constraint Log: CMMI

200. Do you know what your customers expectations are regarding this process?

201. Are there unnecessary steps that are creating bottlenecks and/or causing people to wait?

202. Are best practices and metrics employed to identify issues, progress, performance, etc.?

203. Is there documentation of system capability requirements, data requirements, environment requirements, security requirements, and computer and hardware requirements?

204. How many CMMI project staff does this specific process affect?

205. How do you design an auditing system?

206. Is there a Steering Committee in place?

207. Does a documented CMMI project organizational policy & plan (i.e. governance model) exist?

208. Does the system design reflect the requirements?

209. Can you perform this task or activity in a more effective manner?

210. After observing execution of process, is it in

compliance with the documented Plan?

211. Are processes for release management of new development from coding and unit testing, to integration testing, to training, and production defined and followed?

212. Is this model reasonable?

213. Are there nonconformance issues?

214. What worked well?

215. No superfluous information or marketing narrative?

216. Can the requirements be traced to the appropriate components of the solution, as well as test scripts?

217. Are formal code reviews conducted?

218. Violation trace: why ?

2.8 Work Breakdown Structure: CMMI

219. How many levels?

220. How far down?

221. Is it still viable?

222. Can you make it?

223. Who has to do it?

224. When do you stop?

225. When does it have to be done?

226. Why is it useful?

227. What is the probability of completing the CMMI project in less that xx days?

228. What has to be done?

229. What is the probability that the CMMI project duration will exceed xx weeks?

230. Do you need another level?

231. Where does it take place?

232. Is the work breakdown structure (wbs) defined and is the scope of the CMMI project clear with assigned deliverable owners?

233. How much detail?

234. When would you develop a Work Breakdown Structure?

2.9 WBS Dictionary: CMMI

235. Are all elements of indirect expense identified to overhead cost budgets of CMMI projections?

236. Are internal budgets for authorized, and not priced changes based on the contractors resource plan for accomplishing the work?

237. Are overhead costs budgets established on a basis consistent with anticipated direct business base?

238. Appropriate work authorization documents which subdivide the contractual effort and responsibilities, within functional organizations?

239. Are estimates of costs at completion generated in a rational, consistent manner?

240. Budgets assigned to control accounts?

241. Are current budgets resulting from changes to the authorized work and/or internal replanning, reconcilable to original budgets for specified reporting items?

242. Intermediate schedules, as required, which provide a logical sequence from the master schedule to the control account level?

243. The total budget for the contract (including estimates for authorized and unpriced work)?

244. Are retroactive changes to BCWS and BCWP prohibited except for correction of errors or for normal accounting adjustments?

245. Does the contractors system provide for determination of price variance by comparing planned Vs actual commitments?

246. How detailed should a CMMI project get?

247. Time-phased control account budgets?

248. Does the cost accumulation system provide for summarization of indirect costs from the point of allocation to the contract total?

249. Are detailed work packages planned as far in advance as practicable?

250. Budgets assigned to major functional organizations?

251. Where engineering standards or other internal work measurement systems are used, is there a formal relationship between corresponding values and work package budgets?

252. Is work properly classified as measured effort, LOE, or apportioned effort and appropriately separated?

253. Are overhead budgets and costs being handled according to the disclosure statement when applicable, or otherwise properly classified (for example, engineering overhead, IR&D)?

254. Does the contractor have procedures which permit identification of recurring or non-recurring costs as necessary?

2.10 Schedule Management Plan: CMMI

255. Were CMMI project team members involved in the development of activity & task decomposition?

256. Have CMMI project team accountabilities & responsibilities been clearly defined?

257. Goal: is the schedule feasible and at what cost?

258. Are milestone deliverables effectively tracked and compared to CMMI project plan?

259. What tools and techniques will be used to estimate activity resources?

260. Is a process defined for baseline approval and control?

261. Is there a set of procedures defining the scope, procedures, and deliverables defining quality control?

262. Is funded schedule margin reasonable and logically distributed?

263. Have the key elements of a coherent CMMI project management strategy been established?

264. Has the schedule been baselined?

265. How do you manage time?

266. Has the CMMI project scope been baselined?

267. Is there a formal set of procedures supporting Issues Management?

268. Cost / benefit analysis?

269. Are written status reports provided on a designated frequent basis?

270. Are CMMI project team members committed fulltime?

271. Are risk oriented checklists used during risk identification?

272. Are any non-compliance issues that exist due to your organizations practices communicated to your organization?

273. Has a resource management plan been created?

274. Why time management?

2.11 Activity List: CMMI

275. How detailed should a CMMI project get?

276. What is the probability the CMMI project can be completed in xx weeks?

277. What did not go as well?

278. When will the work be performed?

279. What went well?

280. Can you determine the activity that must finish, before this activity can start?

281. Are the required resources available or need to be acquired?

282. For other activities, how much delay can be tolerated?

283. When do the individual activities need to start and finish?

284. What is the total time required to complete the CMMI project if no delays occur?

285. How should ongoing costs be monitored to try to keep the CMMI project within budget?

286. What is your organizations history in doing similar activities?

287. Is there anything planned that does not need to be here?

288. In what sequence?

289. What went wrong?

290. How will it be performed?

291. Where will it be performed?

292. How difficult will it be to do specific activities on this CMMI project?

293. Is infrastructure setup part of your CMMI project?

2.12 Activity Attributes: CMMI

294. What is the general pattern here?

295. What conclusions/generalizations can you draw from this?

296. Is there a trend during the year?

297. Do you feel very comfortable with your prediction?

298. Activity: what is In the Bag?

299. What activity do you think you should spend the most time on?

300. How many resources do you need to complete the work scope within a limit of X number of days?

301. Can you re-assign any activities to another resource to resolve an over-allocation?

302. Why?

303. Does your organization of the data change its meaning?

304. Have constraints been applied to the start and finish milestones for the phases?

305. Time for overtime?

306. Would you consider either of corresponding

activities an outlier?

307. Resource is assigned to?

308. Resources to accomplish the work?

309. Have you identified the Activity Leveling Priority code value on each activity?

310. What is missing?

311. Activity: fair or not fair?

2.13 Milestone List: CMMI

312. Calculate how long can activity be delayed?

313. Legislative effects?

314. What would happen if a delivery of material was one week late?

315. What are your competitors vulnerabilities?

316. When will the CMMI project be complete?

317. Competitive advantages?

318. Reliability of data, plan predictability?

319. Which path is the critical path?

320. How soon can the activity finish?

321. Loss of key staff?

322. What has been done so far?

323. Own known vulnerabilities?

324. What background experience, skills, and strengths does the team bring to your organization?

325. Political effects?

326. Insurmountable weaknesses?

327. Obstacles faced?

328. Describe the industry you are in and the market growth opportunities. What is the market for your technology, product or service?

329. How soon can the activity start?

330. Who will manage the CMMI project on a day-to-day basis?

2.14 Network Diagram: CMMI

331. Are you on time?

332. What controls the start and finish of a job?

333. Where do you schedule uncertainty time?

334. What activities must occur simultaneously with this activity?

335. What is the completion time?

336. What are the Major Administrative Issues?

337. How confident can you be in your milestone dates and the delivery date?

338. If x is long, what would be the completion time if you break x into two parallel parts of y weeks and z weeks?

339. Are the required resources available?

340. Are the gantt chart and/or network diagram updated periodically and used to assess the overall CMMI project timetable?

341. Exercise: what is the probability that the CMMI project duration will exceed xx weeks?

342. What job or jobs could run concurrently?

343. If a current contract exists, can you provide the

vendor name, contract start, and contract expiration date?

344. What can be done concurrently?

345. If the CMMI project network diagram cannot change and you have extra personnel resources, what is the BEST thing to do?

346. What are the Key Success Factors?

347. Where do schedules come from?

348. Will crashing x weeks return more in benefits than it costs?

349. Review the logical flow of the network diagram. Take a look at which activities you have first and then sequence the activities. Do they make sense?

2.15 Activity Resource Requirements: CMMI

350. Organizational Applicability?

351. Anything else?

352. Do you use tools like decomposition and rolling-wave planning to produce the activity list and other outputs?

353. How do you handle petty cash?

354. When does monitoring begin?

355. How many signatures do you require on a check and does this match what is in your policy and procedures?

356. Which logical relationship does the PDM use most often?

357. Are there unresolved issues that need to be addressed?

358. What is the Work Plan Standard?

359. Other support in specific areas?

360. Why do you do that?

361. What are constraints that you might find during the Human Resource Planning process?

2.16 Resource Breakdown Structure: CMMI

362. Who is allowed to see what data about which resources?

363. Goals for the CMMI project. What is each stakeholders desired outcome for the CMMI project?

364. Who delivers the information?

365. What can you do to improve productivity?

366. Who will use the system?

367. Who will be used as a CMMI project team member?

368. Who is allowed to perform which functions?

369. Why is this important?

370. Is predictive resource analysis being done?

371. Why do you do it?

372. How difficult will it be to do specific activities on this CMMI project?

373. Which resources should be in the resource pool?

374. When do they need the information?

375. What is each stakeholders desired outcome for the CMMI project?

2.17 Activity Duration Estimates: CMMI

376. Does a process exist to determine the probability of risk events?

377. What is done after activity duration estimation?

378. Which is a benefit of an analogous CMMI project estimate?

379. Who has the PRIMARY responsibility to solve this problem?

380. Are actual CMMI project results compared with planned or expected results to determine the variance?

381. Are adjustments implemented to correct or prevent defects?

382. Why is there a growing trend in outsourcing, especially in the government?

383. Which types of reports would help provide summary information to senior management?

384. Consider the changes in the job market for information technology workers. How does the job market and current state of the economy affect human resource management?

385. How difficult will it be to do specific activities on

this CMMI project?

386. Which best describes the relationship between standard deviation and risk?

387. What CMMI project was the first to use modern CMMI project management?

388. Write a oneto two-page paper describing your dream team for this CMMI project. What type of people would you want on your team?

389. What are the main processes included in CMMI project quality management?

390. What steps did your organization take to earn this prestigious quality award?

391. Based on , if you need to shorten the duration of the CMMI project, what activity would you try to shorten?

392. What distinguishes one organization from another in this area?

393. Does a process exist to determine the potential loss or gain if risk events occur?

394. What is wrong with this scenario?

395. Will the new application be developed using existing hardware, software, and networks?

2.18 Duration Estimating Worksheet: CMMI

396. Why estimate costs?

397. What utility impacts are there?

398. Define the work as completely as possible. What work will be included in the CMMI project?

399. What questions do you have?

400. Small or large CMMI project?

401. How should ongoing costs be monitored to try to keep the CMMI project within budget?

402. Why estimate time and cost?

403. What work will be included in the CMMI project?

404. When, then?

405. Is this operation cost effective?

406. Does the CMMI project provide innovative ways for stakeholders to overcome obstacles or deliver better outcomes?

407. What is the total time required to complete the CMMI project if no delays occur?

408. How can the CMMI project be displayed

graphically to better visualize the activities?

409. Science = process: remember the scientific method?

410. Value pocket identification & quantification what are value pockets?

411. What are the critical bottleneck activities?

412. Will the CMMI project collaborate with the local community and leverage resources?

2.19 Project Schedule: CMMI

413. Your CMMI project management plan results in a CMMI project schedule that is too long. If the CMMI project network diagram cannot change and you have extra personnel resources, what is the BEST thing to do?

414. What is the most mis-scheduled part of process?

415. Did the CMMI project come in on schedule?

416. How closely did the initial CMMI project Schedule compare with the actual schedule?

417. Did the CMMI project come in under budget?

418. Verify that the update is accurate. Are all remaining durations correct?

419. What is CMMI project management?

420. Is the CMMI project schedule available for all CMMI project team members to review?

421. Are there activities that came from a template or previous CMMI project that are not applicable on this phase of this CMMI project?

422. What does that mean?

423. What is risk?

424. Is CMMI project work proceeding in accordance

with the original CMMI project schedule?

425. Eliminate unnecessary activities. Are there activities that came from a template or previous CMMI project that are not applicable on this phase of this CMMI project?

426. Are the original CMMI project schedule and budget realistic?

427. How do you manage CMMI project Risk?

428. Are key risk mitigation strategies added to the CMMI project schedule?

2.20 Cost Management Plan: CMMI

429. Forecasts – how will the time and resources needed to complete the CMMI project be forecast?

430. Are the results of quality assurance reviews provided to affected groups & individuals?

431. Risk Analysis?

432. Are assumptions being identified, recorded, analyzed, qualified and closed?

433. Cost variances – how will cost variances be identified and corrected?

434. Who should write the PEP?

435. Has a sponsor been identified?

436. Does the business case include how the CMMI project aligns with your organizations strategic goals & objectives?

437. Contracting method – what contracting method is to be used for the contracts?

438. Have lessons learned been conducted after each CMMI project release?

439. Were CMMI project team members involved in the development of activity & task decomposition?

440. Resources – how will human resources be

scheduled during each phase of the CMMI project?

441. Timeline and milestones?

442. Responsibilities – what is the split of responsibilities between the owner and contractors?

443. Does the detailed work plan match the complexity of tasks with the capabilities of personnel?

444. What would the life cycle costs be?

445. Are meeting objectives identified for each meeting?

446. Is the CMMI project sponsor clearly communicating the business case or rationale for why this CMMI project is needed?

447. Personnel with expertise?

448. Weve met your goals?

2.21 Activity Cost Estimates: CMMI

449. How do you allocate indirect costs to activities?

450. Measurable - are the targets measurable?

451. What were things that you did very well and want to do the same again on the next CMMI project?

452. How do you treat administrative costs in the activity inventory?

453. Performance bond should always provide what part of the contract value?

454. Why do you manage cost?

455. What is procurement?

456. Were sponsors and decision makers available when needed outside regularly scheduled meetings?

457. Certification of actual expenditures?

458. Who determines when the contractor is paid?

459. One way to define activities is to consider how organization employees describe jobs to families and friends. You basically want to know, What do you do?

460. Eac -estimate at completion, what is the total job expected to cost?

461. What is CMMI project cost management?

462. What is the last item a CMMI project manager must do to finalize CMMI project close-out?

463. What communication items need improvement?

464. Where can you get activity reports?

465. What is the activity inventory?

466. What procedures are put in place regarding bidding and cost comparisons, if any?

467. How quickly can the task be done with the skills available?

468. Are data needed on characteristics of care?

2.22 Cost Estimating Worksheet: CMMI

469. Identify the timeframe necessary to monitor progress and collect data to determine how the selected measure has changed?

470. What costs are to be estimated?

471. Who is best positioned to know and assist in identifying corresponding factors?

472. Does the CMMI project provide innovative ways for stakeholders to overcome obstacles or deliver better outcomes?

473. What is the purpose of estimating?

474. What additional CMMI project(s) could be initiated as a result of this CMMI project?

475. Will the CMMI project collaborate with the local community and leverage resources?

476. What will others want?

477. How will the results be shared and to whom?

478. What info is needed?

479. What happens to any remaining funds not used?

480. Can a trend be established from historical

performance data on the selected measure and are the criteria for using trend analysis or forecasting methods met?

481. Ask: are others positioned to know, are others credible, and will others cooperate?

482. Is it feasible to establish a control group arrangement?

483. What can be included?

484. What is the estimated labor cost today based upon this information?

485. Is the CMMI project responsive to community need?

2.23 Cost Baseline: CMMI

486. How difficult will it be to do specific tasks on the CMMI project?

487. Has the CMMI project documentation been archived or otherwise disposed as described in the CMMI project communication plan?

488. Has the appropriate access to relevant data and analysis capability been granted?

489. Are there contingencies or conditions related to the acceptance?

490. Have all approved changes to the schedule baseline been identified and impact on the CMMI project documented?

491. Does it impact schedule, cost, quality?

492. What can go wrong?

493. What does a good WBS NOT look like?

494. How long are you willing to wait before you find out were late?

495. Has the CMMI project (or CMMI project phase) been evaluated against each objective established in the product description and Integrated CMMI project Plan?

496. What strengths do you have?

497. How do you manage cost?

498. Review your risk triggers -have your risks changed?

499. Verify business objectives. Are others appropriate, and well-articulated?

500. Escalation criteria met?

501. How likely is it to go wrong?

502. What deliverables come first?

503. Has training and knowledge transfer of the operations organization been completed?

504. CMMI project goals -should others be reconsidered?

2.24 Quality Management Plan: CMMI

505. How does your organization manage work to promote cooperation, individual initiative, innovation, flexibility, communications, and knowledge/skill sharing across work units?

506. Why quality management?

507. How do your action plans support the strategic objectives?

508. Are you following the quality standards?

509. How is staff trained on the recording of field notes?

510. Who is approving the QAPP?

511. Have adequate resources been provided by management to ensure CMMI project success?

512. What are your organizations key processes (product, service, business, and support)?

513. Are there trends or hot spots?

514. What type of in-house testing do you conduct?

515. Where do you focus?

516. How do you field-modify testing procedures?

517. What would be the next steps or what else

should you do at this point?

518. Is there a Quality Management Plan?

519. With the five whys method, the team considers why the issue being explored occurred. do others then take that initial answer and ask why?

520. How are calibration records kept?

521. Account for the procedures used to verify the data quality of the data being reviewed?

2.25 Quality Metrics: CMMI

522. How should customers provide input?

523. Is there alignment within your organization on definitions?

524. Which data do others need in one place to target areas of improvement?

525. Do you know how much profit a 10% decrease in waste would generate?

526. How do you know if everyone is trying to improve the right things?

527. What forces exist that would cause them to change?

528. Has risk analysis been adequately reviewed?

529. What makes a visualization memorable?

530. Do the operators focus on determining; is there anything you need to worry about?

531. Who is willing to lead?

532. Are quality metrics defined?

533. Has trace of defects been initiated?

534. How is it being measured?

535. If the defect rate during testing is substantially higher than that of the previous release (or a similar product), then ask: Did you plan for and actually improve testing effectiveness?

536. Were number of defects identified?

537. Is material complete (and does it meet the standards)?

538. Did evaluation start on time?

539. How do you communicate results and findings to upper management?

540. How exactly do you define when differences exist?

541. What is the benchmark?

2.26 Process Improvement Plan: CMMI

542. Where do you want to be?

543. To elicit goal statements, do you ask a question such as, What do you want to achieve?

544. Are there forms and procedures to collect and record the data?

545. Who should prepare the process improvement action plan?

546. If a process improvement framework is being used, which elements will help the problems and goals listed?

547. Purpose of goal: the motive is determined by asking, why do you want to achieve this goal?

548. What is the return on investment?

549. What actions are needed to address the problems and achieve the goals?

550. Are you making progress on the goals?

551. Where are you now?

552. What personnel are the coaches for your initiative?

553. Are you meeting the quality standards?

554. What makes people good SPI coaches?

555. How do you measure?

556. What is the test-cycle concept?

557. What personnel are the champions for the initiative?

558. Has a process guide to collect the data been developed?

559. Have the frequency of collection and the points in the process where measurements will be made been determined?

560. What personnel are the sponsors for that initiative?

2.27 Responsibility Assignment Matrix: CMMI

561. Contract line items and end items?

562. Are management actions taken to reduce indirect costs when there are significant adverse variances?

563. Authorization to proceed with all authorized work?

564. Identify potential or actual overruns and underruns?

565. Changes in the overhead pool and/or organization structures?

566. Evaluate the performance of operating organizations?

567. What will the work cost?

568. Do you know how your people are allocated?

569. Do you need to convince people that its well worth the time and effort?

570. Are data elements reconcilable between internal summary reports and reports forwarded to stakeholders?

571. Are the bases and rates for allocating costs from

each indirect pool consistently applied?

572. With too many people labeled as doing the work, are there too many hands involved?

573. The already stated responsible for overhead performance control of related costs?

574. Are indirect costs accumulated for comparison with the corresponding budgets?

575. What tool can show you individual and group allocations?

576. Identify potential or actual budget-based and time-based schedule variances?

577. Competencies and craftsmanship – what competencies are necessary and what level?

2.28 Roles and Responsibilities: CMMI

578. What should you do now to ensure that you are exceeding expectations and excelling in your current position?

579. Concern: where are you limited or have no authority, where you can not influence?

580. Is there a training program in place for stakeholders covering expectations, roles and responsibilities and any addition knowledge others need to be good stakeholders?

581. What expectations were met?

582. Is the data complete?

583. What is working well?

584. Who is responsible for implementation activities and where will the functions, roles and responsibilities be defined?

585. What should you do now to ensure that you are meeting all expectations of your current position?

586. What should you highlight for improvement?

587. Does the team have access to and ability to use data analysis tools?

588. Do the values and practices inherent in the culture of your organization foster or hinder the

process?

589. How well did the CMMI project Team understand the expectations of specific roles and responsibilities?

590. What expectations were NOT met?

591. What areas of supervision are challenging for you?

592. What is working well within your organizations performance management system?

593. Are CMMI project team roles and responsibilities identified and documented?

594. What specific behaviors did you observe?

595. How is your work-life balance?

596. Once the responsibilities are defined for the CMMI project, have the deliverables, roles and responsibilities been clearly communicated to every participant?

2.29 Human Resource Management Plan: CMMI

597. Is there a formal process for updating the CMMI project baseline?

598. Are corrective actions and variances reported?

599. Are milestone deliverables effectively tracked and compared to CMMI project plan?

600. Are meeting minutes captured and sent out after the meeting?

601. Who will be impacted (both positively and negatively) as a result of or during the execution of this CMMI project?

602. How do you determine what key skills and talents are needed to meet the objectives. Is your organization primarily focused on a specific industry?

603. Was the scope definition used in task sequencing?

604. Have all documents been archived in a CMMI project repository for each release?

605. Are all vendor contracts closed out?

606. Do CMMI project managers participating in the CMMI project know the CMMI projects true status first hand?

607. What commitments have been made?

608. Are CMMI project team members committed fulltime?

609. Have CMMI project success criteria been defined?

610. Does the CMMI project have a Statement of Work?

611. Have external dependencies been captured in the schedule?

612. What is the boss?

613. Has a provision been made to reassess CMMI project risks at various CMMI project stages?

614. What is this CMMI project aiming to achieve?

615. Does the schedule include CMMI project management time and change request analysis time?

2.30 Communications Management Plan: CMMI

616. How will the person responsible for executing the communication item be notified?

617. What is the stakeholders level of authority?

618. Are the stakeholders getting the information others need, are others consulted, are concerns addressed?

619. How did the term stakeholder originate?

620. Who is responsible?

621. Are there common objectives between the team and the stakeholder?

622. Are there potential barriers between the team and the stakeholder?

623. What is CMMI project communications management?

624. What approaches do you use?

625. How were corresponding initiatives successful?

626. What communications method?

627. Who will use or be affected by the result of a CMMI project?

628. Which team member will work with each stakeholder?

629. What approaches to you feel are the best ones to use?

630. What does the stakeholder need from the team?

631. Are others part of the communications management plan?

632. Which stakeholders are thought leaders, influences, or early adopters?

633. Who were proponents/opponents?

634. Why is stakeholder engagement important?

2.31 Risk Management Plan: CMMI

635. Are some people working on multiple CMMI projects?

636. Where are you confronted with risks during the business phases?

637. Does the software engineering team have the right mix of skills?

638. Are you working on the right risks?

639. Which is an input to the risk management process?

640. Are end-users enthusiastically committed to the CMMI project and the system/product to be built?

641. Does the CMMI project have the authority and ability to avoid the risk?

642. Was an original risk assessment/risk management plan completed?

643. Are CMMI project requirements stable?

644. Risk probability and impact: how will the probabilities and impacts of risk items be assessed?

645. Are the best people available?

646. Are staff committed for the duration of the product?

647. What is the likelihood that your organization would accept responsibility for the risk?

648. Havent software CMMI projects been late before?

649. Who/what can assist?

650. Is the process being followed?

651. How are risk analvsis and prioritization performed?

652. Is security a central objective?

2.32 Risk Register: CMMI

653. Are your objectives at risk?

654. What would the impact to the CMMI project objectives be should the risk arise?

655. Can the likelihood and impact of failing to achieve corresponding recommendations and action plans be assessed?

656. What is the appropriate level of risk management for this CMMI project?

657. What action, if any, has been taken to respond to the risk?

658. Have other controls and solutions been implemented in other services which could be applied as an alternative to additional funding?

659. Are there other alternative controls that could be implemented?

660. When is it going to be done?

661. What should you do when?

662. How well are risks controlled?

663. What should the audit role be in establishing a risk management process?

664. Technology risk -is the CMMI project technically

feasible?

665. When will it happen?

666. What risks might negatively or positively affect achieving the CMMI project objectives?

667. Which key risks have ineffective responses or outstanding improvement actions?

668. Is further information required before making a decision?

669. What can be done about it?

670. Market risk -will the new service or product be useful to your organization or marketable to others?

2.33 Probability and Impact Assessment: CMMI

671. Are there any CMMI projects similar to this one in existence?

672. Do you use any methods to analyze risks?

673. Have customers been involved fully in the definition of requirements?

674. What is the likelihood?

675. What kind of preparation would be required to do this?

676. What is the experience (performance, attitude, business ethics, etc.) in the past with contractors?

677. Which role do you have in the CMMI project?

678. What are the channels available for distribution to the customer?

679. What are the chances the event will occur?

680. What is the probability of the risk occurring?

681. Which functions, departments, and activities of your organization are going to be affected?

682. Is the customer technically sophisticated in the product area?

683. Should the risk be taken at all?

684. What can you do about it?

685. Are staff committed for the duration of the CMMI project?

686. What will be the impact or consequence if the risk occurs?

687. Are tools for analysis and design available?

688. What should be the level of coordination?

689. How much is the probability of a risk occurring?

2.34 Probability and Impact Matrix: CMMI

690. Who is going to be the consortium leader?

691. How is the risk management process used in practice?

692. What changes in the regulation are forthcoming?

693. Have you ascribed a level of confidence to every critical technical objective?

694. Are some people working on multiple CMMI projects?

695. Brain storm – mind maps, what if?

696. Who has experience with this?

697. How do you analyze the risks in the different types of CMMI projects?

698. How likely is the current plan to come in on schedule or on budget?

699. What are the levels of understanding of the future users of this technology?

700. Risk categorization -which of your categories has more risk than others?

701. What risks are necessary to achieve success?

702. What are data sources?

703. What should be the level of difficulty in handling the technology?

704. What do you expect?

705. Do others match with the clients requirement?

706. How do you define a risk?

707. How would you define a risk?

2.35 Risk Data Sheet: CMMI

708. What are the main opportunities available to you that you should grab while you can?

709. How reliable is the data source?

710. Potential for recurrence?

711. What actions can be taken to eliminate or remove risk?

712. What are your core values?

713. What is the environment within which you operate (social trends, economic, community values, broad based participation, national directions etc.)?

714. Do effective diagnostic tests exist?

715. If it happens, what are the consequences?

716. What is the chance that it will happen?

717. How can hazards be reduced?

718. Has a sensitivity analysis been carried out?

719. What are you here for (Mission)?

720. Risk of what?

721. What do people affected think about the need for, and practicality of preventive measures?

722. Type of risk identified?

723. What will be the consequences if the risk happens?

724. What will be the consequences if it happens?

725. What can you do?

726. What was measured?

727. Whom do you serve (customers)?

2.36 Procurement Management Plan: CMMI

728. Are changes in scope (deliverable commitments) agreed to by all affected groups & individuals?

729. Have the procedures for identifying budget variances been followed?

730. How will you coordinate Procurement with aspects of the CMMI project?

731. Are all payments made according to the contract(s)?

732. Is the assigned CMMI project manager a PMP (Certified CMMI project manager) and experienced?

733. Are target dates established for each milestone deliverable?

734. Are estimating assumptions and constraints captured?

735. Does a documented CMMI project organizational policy & plan (i.e. governance model) exist?

736. Public engagement – did you get it right?

737. Does the CMMI project have a Statement of Work?

738. Are meeting minutes captured and sent out after

meetings?

739. Is an industry recognized mechanized support tool(s) being used for CMMI project scheduling & tracking?

740. Do you have the reasons why the changes to your organizational systems and capabilities are required?

741. Is a payment system in place with proper reviews and approvals?

742. Are status reports received per the CMMI project Plan?

743. Is it possible to track all classes of CMMI project work (e.g. scheduled, un-scheduled, defect repair, etc.)?

744. Is there general agreement & acceptance of the current status and progress of the CMMI project?

2.37 Source Selection Criteria: CMMI

745. Are there any common areas of weaknesses or deficiencies in the proposals in the competitive range?

746. How do you consolidate reviews and analysis of evaluators?

747. How are clarifications and communications appropriately used?

748. Do you prepare an independent cost estimate?

749. Who must be notified?

750. What should be considered when developing evaluation standards?

751. How important is cost in the source selection decision relative to past performance and technical considerations?

752. Comparison of each offers prices to the estimated prices -are there significant differences?

753. What can not be disclosed?

754. When is it appropriate to issue a Draft Request for Proposal (DRFP)?

755. Can you prevent comparison of proposals?

756. How can the methods of publicizing the buy be

tailored to yield more effective price competition?

757. Are types/quantities of material, facilities appropriate?

758. How should oral presentations be prepared for?

759. Who is entitled to a debriefing?

760. In the technical/management area, what criteria do you use to determine the final evaluation ratings?

761. How should the preproposal conference be conducted?

762. Who should attend debriefings?

763. What should clarifications include?

764. What should be considered?

2.38 Stakeholder Management Plan: CMMI

765. Were CMMI project team members involved in the development of activity & task decomposition?

766. Are metrics used to evaluate and manage Vendors?

767. Are the appropriate IT resources adequate to meet planned commitments?

768. How are you doing/what can be done better?

769. Are regulatory inspections considered part of quality control?

770. Is there a formal process for updating the CMMI project baseline?

771. Do CMMI project teams & team members report on status / activities / progress?

772. Are schedule deliverables actually delivered?

773. Who is gathering information?

774. Who is responsible for accepting the reports produced by the process?

775. Was your organizations estimating methodology being used and followed?

776. Were the budget estimates reasonable?

777. Will CMMI project success require up to date information at a moments notice?

778. What are the procedures and processes to be followed for purchases, including approval and authorisation requirements?

779. Describe the process that will be used to design, develop, review, accept, distribute and change outputs. Will all outputs delivered by the CMMI project follow the same process?

780. Are decisions captured in a decisions log?

781. Have activity relationships and interdependencies within tasks been adequately identified?

782. Have reserves been created to address risks?

783. What is the drawback in using qualitative CMMI project selection techniques?

2.39 Change Management Plan: CMMI

784. What relationships will change?

785. What prerequisite knowledge do corresponding groups need?

786. Who in the business it includes?

787. Who might be able to help you the most?

788. What will be the preferred method of delivery?

789. When should a given message be communicated?

790. Impact of systems implementation on organization change?

791. What is the negative impact of communicating too soon or too late?

792. What are the needs, priorities and special interests of the audience?

793. What is the most positive interpretation it can receive?

794. Who might present the most resistance?

795. Who is the target audience of the piece of information?

796. What are the essentials of the message?

797. What skills, education, knowledge, or work experiences should the resources have for each identified competency?

798. What are the training strategies?

799. Who will be the change levers?

800. How does the principle of senders and receivers make the CMMI project communications effort more complex?

801. When does it make sense to customize?

802. Has this been negotiated with the customer and sponsor?

803. Has the training co-ordinator been provided with the training details and put in place the necessary arrangements?

3.0 Executing Process Group: CMMI

804. Is the program supported by national and/or local organizations?

805. Could a new application negatively affect the current IT infrastructure?

806. Specific - is the objective clear in terms of what, how, when, and where the situation will be changed?

807. What are the typical CMMI project management skills?

808. What are the critical steps involved with strategy mapping?

809. What are some crucial elements of a good CMMI project plan?

810. How can your organization use a weighted decision matrix to evaluate proposals as part of source selection?

811. Is activity definition the first process involved in CMMI project time management?

812. Is the CMMI project making progress in helping to achieve the set results?

813. How do you measure difficulty?

814. What is involved in the solicitation process?

815. What areas were overlooked on this CMMI project?

816. How does the job market and current state of the economy affect human resource management?

817. What were things that you did very well and want to do the same again on the next CMMI project?

818. Does the case present a realistic scenario?

819. Is the schedule for the set products being met?

820. What areas does the group agree are the biggest success on the CMMI project?

821. How do you control progress of your CMMI project?

822. In what way has the program come up with innovative measures for problem-solving?

3.1 Team Member Status Report: CMMI

823. Does the product, good, or service already exist within your organization?

824. Does every department have to have a CMMI project Manager on staff?

825. Will the staff do training or is that done by a third party?

826. The problem with Reward & Recognition Programs is that the truly deserving people all too often get left out. How can you make it practical?

827. Do you have an Enterprise CMMI project Management Office (EPMO)?

828. What is to be done?

829. What specific interest groups do you have in place?

830. How will resource planning be done?

831. How it is to be done?

832. How can you make it practical?

833. How does this product, good, or service meet the needs of the CMMI project and your organization as a whole?

834. Are the attitudes of staff regarding CMMI project work improving?

835. How much risk is involved?

836. Why is it to be done?

837. Does your organization have the means (staff, money, contract, etc.) to produce or to acquire the product, good, or service?

838. Are your organizations CMMI projects more successful over time?

839. Is there evidence that staff is taking a more professional approach toward management of your organizations CMMI projects?

840. When a teams productivity and success depend on collaboration and the efficient flow of information, what generally fails them?

841. Are the products of your organizations CMMI projects meeting customers objectives?

3.2 Change Request: CMMI

842. What is the relationship between requirements attributes and attributes like complexity and size?

843. Customer acceptance plan how will the customer verify the change has been implemented successfully?

844. Screen shots or attachments included in a Change Request?

845. Are you implementing itil processes?

846. Have all related configuration items been properly updated?

847. Who is communicating the change?

848. What is the change request log?

849. Should staff call into the helpdesk or go to the website?

850. Will all change requests and current status be logged?

851. How is quality being addressed on the CMMI project?

852. What is the purpose of change control?

853. How well do experienced software developers predict software change?

854. What kind of information about the change request needs to be captured?

855. How are changes requested (forms, method of communication)?

856. How many times must the change be modified or presented to the change control board before it is approved?

857. Which requirements attributes affect the risk to reliability the most?

858. Have scm procedures for noting the change, recording it, and reporting it been followed?

859. Who can suggest changes?

860. Has a formal technical review been conducted to assess technical correctness?

861. Why were your requested changes rejected or not made?

3.3 Change Log: CMMI

862. Is this a mandatory replacement?

863. Should a more thorough impact analysis be conducted?

864. Is the requested change request a result of changes in other CMMI project(s)?

865. How does this change affect the timeline of the schedule?

866. When was the request submitted?

867. When was the request approved?

868. Is the change request within CMMI project scope?

869. How does this relate to the standards developed for specific business processes?

870. Does the suggested change request represent a desired enhancement to the products functionality?

871. Do the described changes impact on the integrity or security of the system?

872. Where do changes come from?

873. How does this change affect scope?

874. Is the submitted change a new change or a

modification of a previously approved change?

875. Is the change request open, closed or pending?

876. Who initiated the change request?

877. Does the suggested change request seem to represent a necessary enhancement to the product?

878. Is the change backward compatible without limitations?

879. Will the CMMI project fail if the change request is not executed?

3.4 Decision Log: CMMI

880. What makes you different or better than others companies selling the same thing?

881. How does an increasing emphasis on cost containment influence the strategies and tactics used?

882. Is everything working as expected?

883. Adversarial environment. is your opponent open to a non-traditional workflow, or will it likely challenge anything you do?

884. Does anything need to be adjusted?

885. With whom was the decision shared or considered?

886. Meeting purpose; why does this team meet?

887. How does provision of information, both in terms of content and presentation, influence acceptance of alternative strategies?

888. How do you define success?

889. Decision-making process; how will the team make decisions?

890. How effective is maintaining the log at facilitating organizational learning?

891. Who will be given a copy of this document and where will it be kept?

892. What is your overall strategy for quality control / quality assurance procedures?

893. Linked to original objective?

894. How do you know when you are achieving it?

895. Behaviors; what are guidelines that the team has identified that will assist them with getting the most out of team meetings?

896. What eDiscovery problem or issue did your organization set out to fix or make better?

897. What was the rationale for the decision?

898. Which variables make a critical difference?

899. It becomes critical to track and periodically revisit both operational effectiveness; Are you noticing all that you need to, and are you interpreting what you see effectively?

3.5 Quality Audit: CMMI

900. What are you trying to accomplish with this audit?

901. How does your organization know that its staffing profile is optimally aligned with the capability requirements implicit (or explicit) in its Strategic Plan?

902. Are all complaints involving the possible failure of a device, labeling, or packaging to meet any of its specifications reviewed, evaluated, and investigated?

903. What does an analysis of your organizations staff profile suggest in terms of its planning, and how is this being addressed?

904. How does your organization know that it is maintaining a conducive staff climate?

905. Do prior clients have a positive opinion of your organization?

906. Are the intentions consistent with external obligations (such as applicable laws)?

907. How does your organization know that the range and quality of its social and recreational services and facilities are appropriately effective and constructive in meeting the needs of staff?

908. What does the organizarion look for in a Quality audit?

909. How does your organization know that its research planning and management systems are appropriately effective and constructive in enabling quality research outcomes?

910. How does your organization know that its management of its ethical responsibilities is appropriately effective and constructive?

911. How does the organization know that its industry and community engagement planning and management systems are appropriately effective and constructive in enabling relationships with key stakeholder groups?

912. How does your organization know that its system for recruiting the best staff possible are appropriately effective and constructive?

913. Is there a written procedure for receiving materials?

914. How does your organization know that its staff have appropriate access to a fair and effective grievance process?

915. Is there a written corporate quality policy?

916. Are all employees made aware of device defects which may occur from the improper performance of specific jobs?

917. How does your organization know that its system for ensuring a positive organizational climate is appropriately effective and constructive?

918. For each device to be reconditioned, are device specifications, such as appropriate engineering drawings, component specifications and software specifications, maintained?

919. Is quality audit a prerequisite for program accreditation or program recognition?

3.6 Team Directory: CMMI

920. Is construction on schedule?

921. What needs to be communicated?

922. Who will write the meeting minutes and distribute?

923. What are you going to deliver or accomplish?

924. How will you accomplish and manage the objectives?

925. Who will talk to the customer?

926. Have you decided when to celebrate the CMMI projects completion date?

927. How and in what format should information be presented?

928. Process decisions: is work progressing on schedule and per contract requirements?

929. Who are your stakeholders (customers, sponsors, end users, team members)?

930. Does a CMMI project team directory list all resources assigned to the CMMI project?

931. Process decisions: how well was task order work performed?

932. Contract requirements complied with?

933. Decisions: what could be done better to improve the quality of the constructed product?

934. Process decisions: do invoice amounts match accepted work in place?

935. Who are the Team Members?

936. When will you produce deliverables?

937. Where will the product be used and/or delivered or built when appropriate?

938. Who will report CMMI project status to all stakeholders?

3.7 Team Operating Agreement: CMMI

939. Are team roles clearly defined and accepted?

940. Do you vary your voice pace, tone and pitch to engage participants and gain involvement?

941. Do you post any action items, due dates, and responsibilities on the team website?

942. Must your members collaborate successfully to complete CMMI projects?

943. Do you brief absent members after they view meeting notes or listen to a recording?

944. Do you leverage technology engagement tools group chat, polls, screen sharing, etc.?

945. Confidentiality: how will confidential information be handled?

946. Do you ensure that all participants know how to use the required technology?

947. What are the boundaries (organizational or geographic) within which you operate?

948. Do you listen for voice tone and word choice to understand the meaning behind words?

949. What is the anticipated procedure (recruitment, solicitation of volunteers, or assignment) for selecting team members?

950. What is the number of cases currently teamed?

951. Do team members reside in more than two countries?

952. Are there more than two national cultures represented by your team?

953. How will you resolve conflict efficiently and respectfully?

954. Did you delegate tasks such as taking meeting minutes, presenting a topic and soliciting input?

955. Did you determine the technology methods that best match the messages to be communicated?

956. What is group supervision?

957. How do you want to be thought of and known within your organization?

3.8 Team Performance Assessment: CMMI

958. How does CMMI project termination impact CMMI project team members?

959. To what degree can team members meet frequently enough to accomplish the teams ends?

960. To what degree is there a sense that only the team can succeed?

961. If you have received criticism from reviewers that your work suffered from method variance, what was the circumstance?

962. Do you promptly inform members about major developments that may affect them?

963. What structural changes have you made or are you preparing to make?

964. Can team performance be reliably measured in simulator and live exercises using the same assessment tool?

965. To what degree does the teams approach to its work allow for modification and improvement over time?

966. How hard did you try to make a good selection?

967. To what degree do team members articulate the

teams work approach?

968. To what degree is the team cognizant of small wins to be celebrated along the way?

969. Do friends perform better than acquaintances?

970. To what degree do members understand and articulate the same purpose without relying on ambiguous abstractions?

971. To what degree are corresponding categories of skills either actually or potentially represented across the membership?

972. To what degree can all members engage in open and interactive considerations?

973. Effects of crew composition on crew performance: Does the whole equal the sum of its parts?

974. Delaying market entry: how long is too long?

975. If you have criticized someones work for method variance in your role as reviewer, what was the circumstance?

976. What is method variance?

977. Can familiarity breed backup?

3.9 Team Member Performance Assessment: CMMI

978. What is collaboration?

979. Are assessment validation activities performed?

980. What were the challenges that resulted for training and assessment?

981. Does the rater (supervisor) have the authority or responsibility to tell an employee that the employees performance is unsatisfactory?

982. How do you currently account for your results in the teams achievement?

983. Why were corresponding selected?

984. Are the draft goals SMART ?

985. What does collaboration look like?

986. To what degree do team members feel that the purpose of the team is important, if not exciting?

987. To what degree does the teams purpose contain themes that are particularly meaningful and memorable?

988. Do the goals support your organizations goals?

989. What are best practices for delivering and

developing training evaluations to maximize the benefits of leveraging emerging technologies?

990. How do you make use of research?

991. To what degree are the relative importance and priority of the goals clear to all team members?

992. Should a ratee get a copy of all the raters documents about the employees performance?

993. Who should attend?

994. To what degree do team members frequently explore the teams purpose and its implications?

995. Does statute or regulation require the job responsibility?

996. What variables that affect team members achievement are within your control?

3.10 Issue Log: CMMI

997. What help do you and your team need from the stakeholders?

998. Is there an important stakeholder who is actively opposed and will not receive messages?

999. How often do you engage with stakeholders?

1000. Who is the issue assigned to?

1001. Who reported the issue?

1002. What would have to change?

1003. What is the stakeholders political influence?

1004. Who needs to know and how much?

1005. In your work, how much time is spent on stakeholder identification?

1006. How is this initiative related to other portfolios, programs, or CMMI projects?

1007. Is access to the Issue Log controlled?

1008. Do you often overlook a key stakeholder or stakeholder group?

1009. Do you prepare stakeholder engagement plans?

1010. Are you constantly rushing from meeting to

meeting?

1011. Are stakeholder roles recognized by your organization?

1012. Do you feel more overwhelmed by stakeholders?

4.0 Monitoring and Controlling Process Group: CMMI

1013. What is the timeline?

1014. How can you make your needs known?

1015. How well did the team follow the chosen processes?

1016. How well did the chosen processes produce the expected results?

1017. When will the CMMI project be done?

1018. How well defined and documented were the CMMI project management processes you chose to use?

1019. Key stakeholders to work with. How many potential communications channels exist on the CMMI project?

1020. Just how important is your work to the overall success of the CMMI project?

1021. If action is called for, what form should it take?

1022. How is agile portfolio management done?

1023. How is agile CMMI project management done?

1024. Are the necessary foundations in place

to ensure the sustainability of the results of the programme?

1025. Are there areas that need improvement?

1026. Is there undesirable impact on staff or resources?

1027. How can you monitor progress?

1028. Were escalated issues resolved promptly?

1029. Is progress on outcomes due to your program?

4.1 Project Performance Report: CMMI

1030. To what degree do individual skills and abilities match task demands?

1031. What is the degree to which rules govern information exchange between groups?

1032. To what degree will new and supplemental skills be introduced as the need is recognized?

1033. To what degree does the information network communicate information relevant to the task?

1034. To what degree are sub-teams possible or necessary?

1035. How is the data used?

1036. To what degree does the formal organization make use of individual resources and meet individual needs?

1037. To what degree does the team possess adequate membership to achieve its ends?

1038. To what degree can the cognitive capacity of individuals accommodate the flow of information?

1039. To what degree does the teams work approach provide opportunity for members to engage in open interaction?

1040. To what degree will team members, individually and collectively, commit time to help themselves and others learn and develop skills?

1041. To what degree are the teams goals and objectives clear, simple, and measurable?

1042. To what degree is there centralized control of information sharing?

1043. To what degree do members articulate the goals beyond the team membership?

1044. What degree are the relative importance and priority of the goals clear to all team members?

1045. To what degree will the team ensure that all members equitably share the work essential to the success of the team?

1046. To what degree are the goals realistic?

1047. To what degree is the information network consistent with the structure of the formal organization?

4.2 Variance Analysis: CMMI

1048. Are the requirements for all items of overhead established by rational, traceable processes?

1049. Is the market likely to continue to grow at this rate next year?

1050. Are there knowledgeable CMMI projections of future performance?

1051. How do you identify and isolate causes of favorable and unfavorable cost and schedule variances?

1052. How do you manage changes in the nature of the overhead requirements?

1053. Are there externalities from having some customers, even if they are unprofitable in the short run?

1054. Did a new competitor enter the market?

1055. Is data disseminated to the contractors management timely, accurate, and usable?

1056. What is the budgeted cost for work scheduled?

1057. What is the performance to date and material commitment?

1058. When, during the last four quarters, did a primary business event occur causing a fluctuation?

1059. What was the cause of the increase in costs?

1060. What are the direct labor dollars and/or hours?

1061. How are material, labor, and overhead variances calculated and recorded?

1062. Are the overhead pools formally and adequately identified?

1063. How do you verify authorization to proceed with all authorized work?

1064. What are the actual costs to date?

1065. What should management do?

4.3 Earned Value Status: CMMI

1066. Where is evidence-based earned value in your organization reported?

1067. Validation is a process of ensuring that the developed system will actually achieve the stakeholders desired outcomes; Are you building the right product? What do you validate?

1068. Where are your problem areas?

1069. When is it going to finish?

1070. Are you hitting your CMMI projects targets?

1071. How does this compare with other CMMI projects?

1072. If earned value management (EVM) is so good in determining the true status of a CMMI project and CMMI project its completion, why is it that hardly any one uses it in information systems related CMMI projects?

1073. Earned value can be used in almost any CMMI project situation and in almost any CMMI project environment. it may be used on large CMMI projects, medium sized CMMI projects, tiny CMMI projects (in cut-down form), complex and simple CMMI projects and in any market sector. some people, of course, know all about earned value, they have used it for years - but perhaps not as effectively as they could have?

1074. Verification is a process of ensuring that the developed system satisfies the stakeholders agreements and specifications; Are you building the product right? What do you verify?

1075. What is the unit of forecast value?

1076. How much is it going to cost by the finish?

4.4 Risk Audit: CMMI

1077. Improving fraud detection: do auditors react to abnormal inconsistencies between financial and non-financial measures?

1078. Are risk management strategies documented?

1079. Does your organization have a process for meeting its ongoing taxation obligations?

1080. If applicable; are compilers and code generators available and suitable for the product to be built?

1081. Do you have a realistic budget and do you present regular financial reports that identify how you are going against that budget?

1082. Is the customer willing to participate in reviews?

1083. Does your auditor understand your business?

1084. What are the Internal Controls ?

1085. Do you meet the legislative requirements (for example PAYG, super contributions) for paid employees?

1086. Are testing tools available and suitable?

1087. What compliance systems do you have in place to address quality, errors, and outcomes?

1088. From an empirical perspective, does the

business risk approach lead to a more effective audit, or simply to increased consulting revenue detrimental to audit rigor?

1089. What programmatic and Fiscal information is being collected and analyzed?

1090. Are team members trained in the use of the tools?

1091. Do all coaches/instructors/leaders have appropriate and current accreditation?

1092. Does your organization have a social media policy and procedure?

1093. Do you have position descriptions for all key paid and volunteer positions in your organization?

1094. What does monitoring consist of?

1095. For this risk .. what do you need to stop doing, start doing and keep doing?

4.5 Contractor Status Report: CMMI

1096. What was the final actual cost?

1097. How does the proposed individual meet each requirement?

1098. How is risk transferred?

1099. If applicable; describe your standard schedule for new software version releases. Are new software version releases included in the standard maintenance plan?

1100. What was the overall budget or estimated cost?

1101. Who can list a CMMI project as organization experience, your organization or a previous employee of your organization?

1102. Describe how often regular updates are made to the proposed solution. Are corresponding regular updates included in the standard maintenance plan?

1103. What was the actual budget or estimated cost for your organizations services?

1104. Are there contractual transfer concerns?

1105. What process manages the contracts?

1106. What was the budget or estimated cost for your organizations services?

1107. What are the minimum and optimal bandwidth requirements for the proposed solution?

1108. What is the average response time for answering a support call?

1109. How long have you been using the services?

4.6 Formal Acceptance: CMMI

1110. Does it do what client said it would?

1111. What can you do better next time?

1112. Did the CMMI project achieve its MOV?

1113. Did the CMMI project manager and team act in a professional and ethical manner?

1114. General estimate of the costs and times to complete the CMMI project?

1115. How well did the team follow the methodology?

1116. Who supplies data?

1117. What lessons were learned about your CMMI project management methodology?

1118. Was the client satisfied with the CMMI project results?

1119. Was the CMMI project goal achieved?

1120. Do you perform formal acceptance or burn-in tests?

1121. Do you buy-in installation services?

1122. Have all comments been addressed?

1123. Was the CMMI project work done on time,

within budget, and according to specification?

1124. Was the sponsor/customer satisfied?

1125. What features, practices, and processes proved to be strengths or weaknesses?

1126. Is formal acceptance of the CMMI project product documented and distributed?

1127. What function(s) does it fill or meet?

1128. What is the Acceptance Management Process?

1129. Do you buy pre-configured systems or build your own configuration?

5.0 Closing Process Group: CMMI

1130. If a risk event occurs, what will you do?

1131. What areas does the group agree are the biggest success on the CMMI project?

1132. What will you do to minimize the impact should a risk event occur?

1133. Is this a follow-on to a previous CMMI project?

1134. Was the user/client satisfied with the end product?

1135. What was learned?

1136. What were the desired outcomes?

1137. Is there a clear cause and effect between the activity and the lesson learned?

1138. What were things that you did very well and want to do the same again on the next CMMI project?

1139. Will the CMMI project deliverable(s) replace a current asset or group of assets?

1140. Is this an updated CMMI project Proposal Document?

1141. How well did the chosen processes fit the needs of the CMMI project?

1142. What do you need to do?

1143. Are there funding or time constraints?

1144. Were cost budgets met?

1145. How dependent is the CMMI project on other CMMI projects or work efforts?

5.1 Procurement Audit: CMMI

1146. Was the payment made to the supplier/contractor within the time frames indicated in the contracts?

1147. Did you consider and evaluate alternatives, like bundling needs with other departments or grouping supplies in separate lots with different characteristics?

1148. Are purchasing actions processed on a timely basis?

1149. Are risks in the external environment identified, for example: Budgetary constraints?

1150. Has your organization examined in detail the definition of performance?

1151. Was the chosen procedure the most efficient and effective for the performance of the contract?

1152. Do staff involved in the various stages of the process have the appropriate skills and training to perform duties effectively?

1153. Do established procedures ensure that computer programs will not pay the same group of invoices twice?

1154. Is there management monitoring of transactions and balances?

1155. Are the number of checking accounts where

cash segregation is not required kept to a reasonable number?

1156. Are criteria and sub-criteria set suitable to identify the tender that offers best value for money?

1157. Were the specifications of the contract determined free from influence of particular interests of consultants, experts or other economic operators?

1158. In open and restricted procedures, did the contracting authority make sure that there is no substantive change to the bid due to this clearing process?

1159. Was the tender clearly and properly specified, including evaluation criteria and knowing about the market and therefore not over-prescriptive and receptive to innovation?

1160. Is there a procedure to summarize bids and select a vendor?

1161. Were no charges billed to interested economic operators or the parties to the system?

1162. When corresponding references were made, was a precise description of the performance not otherwise possible and were the already stated references accompanied by the words or equivalent?

1163. Were standards, certifications and evidence required admissible?

1164. Did the bidder comply with requests within the deadline set?

1165. Are incentives to deliver on time and in quantity properly specified?

5.2 Contract Close-Out: CMMI

1166. Are the signers the authorized officials?

1167. Have all contracts been closed?

1168. Parties: who is involved?

1169. Was the contract sufficiently clear so as not to result in numerous disputes and misunderstandings?

1170. How/when used ?

1171. Change in attitude or behavior?

1172. Change in circumstances?

1173. Why Outsource?

1174. Was the contract type appropriate?

1175. What is capture management?

1176. Have all acceptance criteria been met prior to final payment to contractors?

1177. Parties: Authorized?

1178. How does it work?

1179. Have all contracts been completed?

1180. Have all contract records been included in the CMMI project archives?

1181. How is the contracting office notified of the automatic contract close-out?

1182. Has each contract been audited to verify acceptance and delivery?

1183. Change in knowledge?

1184. What happens to the recipient of services?

1185. Was the contract complete without requiring numerous changes and revisions?

5.3 Project or Phase Close-Out: CMMI

1186. How much influence did the stakeholder have over others?

1187. What is this stakeholder expecting?

1188. What are the mandatory communication needs for each stakeholder?

1189. How often did each stakeholder need an update?

1190. Does the lesson describe a function that would be done differently the next time?

1191. In preparing the Lessons Learned report, should it reflect a consensus viewpoint, or should the report reflect the different individual viewpoints?

1192. What can you do better next time, and what specific actions can you take to improve?

1193. What are the marketing communication needs for each stakeholder?

1194. What were the actual outcomes?

1195. If you were the CMMI project sponsor, how would you determine which CMMI project team(s) and/or individuals deserve recognition?

1196. Planned completion date?

1197. What benefits or impacts does the stakeholder group expect to obtain as a result of the CMMI project?

1198. What was the preferred delivery mechanism?

1199. What information is each stakeholder group interested in?

1200. What process was planned for managing issues/risks?

1201. Have business partners been involved extensively, and what data was required for them?

1202. What was expected from each stakeholder?

1203. What could be done to improve the process?

1204. Planned remaining costs?

5.4 Lessons Learned: CMMI

1205. How effective was the quality assurance process?

1206. Did the team work well together?

1207. What report generation capability is needed?

1208. What is the distribution of authority?

1209. If you had to do this CMMI project again, what is the one thing that you would change (related to process, not to technical solutions)?

1210. How much communication is task-related?

1211. What needs to be done over or differently?

1212. How was the political and social history changed over the life of the CMMI project?

1213. What is your organizational ideology?

1214. Would you spend your own money to fix this issue?

1215. How much time is required for the task?

1216. Did the CMMI project change significantly?

1217. What is the economic growth rate?

1218. How efficient is the deliverable?

1219. How smooth do you feel Integration has been?

1220. Are there any data that you have overlooked in identifying lessons?

1221. Will the information remain current?

1222. If issue escalation was required, how effectively were issues resolved?

1223. What is the impact of tax policy?

1224. Who managed most of the communication within the CMMI project?

Index

abilities 243
ability   25, 194, 200
abnormal   249
absent 233
accept   143, 201, 215
acceptable   128, 145
acceptance   6, 88, 103, 145, 184, 211, 222, 226, 253-254, 260-261
accepted   140, 143, 232-233
accepting   143, 214
access 2, 7-9, 101, 184, 194, 229, 239
accomplish   7, 35, 113, 164, 228, 231, 235
accordance   176
according   30, 36, 67, 118, 157, 210, 254
account   23, 50, 54, 85, 124, 156-157, 187, 237
accounted   40
accounting   157
accounts   156, 257
accuracy   41
accurate   9, 36, 84, 146, 176, 245
accurately   44
achievable   47
achieve   7, 62, 98, 104, 106, 109, 126, 139, 190, 197, 202, 206, 218, 243, 247, 253
achieved   18, 51, 253
achieving   81, 138, 203, 227
acquire   221
acquired   66, 161
across   140, 186, 236
action   131, 142, 186, 190, 202, 233, 241
actions 42, 80, 139, 190, 192, 196, 203, 208, 257, 262
actively   239
activities   17, 32, 39, 43, 49-53, 56, 58, 62-63, 76, 82-83, 88, 93-94, 100, 109, 112, 115, 121, 123, 127-128, 144, 161-164, 167-168, 170, 172, 175-177, 180, 194, 204, 214, 237
activity 3-4, 22, 33, 56, 58, 63, 139, 152, 159, 161, 163-167, 169, 172-173, 178, 180-181, 214-215, 218, 255
actual   33, 145, 157, 172, 176, 180, 192-193, 246, 251, 262
actually   36, 60, 189, 214, 236, 247
adding 48

addition 101, 194
additional 30, 59, 145, 182, 202
additions 86
address 23, 25-26, 54, 61, 69, 76, 93, 100, 106-107, 123, 138, 142, 190, 215, 249
addressed 101, 116, 141, 169, 198, 222, 228, 253
addresses 74
addressing 25
adequate 16, 24, 96, 110, 123, 151, 186, 214, 243
adequately 30, 108, 138, 188, 215, 246
adhered 89
adjusted 58, 226
admissible 258
adopters 199
adopting 66, 76, 84, 90, 98, 120, 124
adoption 39-40, 43, 45, 61, 83, 87, 98
advance 157
advantage 120
advantages 124, 136, 146, 165
adverse 192
affect 59, 71, 75, 88, 102, 107, 139, 148, 150, 152, 172, 203, 218-219, 223-224, 235, 238
affected 109, 178, 198, 204, 208, 210
affecting 11, 46
against 27, 42, 184, 249
agenda 138
agendas 142
agreed 40-41, 95-96, 210
Agreement 5, 124, 145, 211, 233
agreements 25, 119, 248
aiming 197
aligned 18, 126, 228
Aligning 105
alignment 28, 30, 188
aligns 178
alleged 1
allocate 180
allocated 192
allocating 192
allocation 51, 157
allowed 170
allows 9
almost 247

already   24, 42, 69, 76, 193, 220, 258
always 9, 180
ambiguous   236
amounts   232
analogous   172
analysis   201
analysis   2, 5, 9-10, 39-40, 42-43, 70-71, 74, 78, 136, 140, 144, 160, 170, 178, 183-184, 188, 194, 197, 205, 208, 212, 224, 228, 245
analytics   43-44
analyze   2, 45-46, 48, 67, 204, 206
analyzed   39, 69, 144, 178, 250
annually   65
another   154, 163, 173
answer 10-11, 15, 21, 38, 48, 60, 65, 79, 92, 187
answered   20, 37, 47, 63, 78, 90, 124, 129
answering   10, 252
anticipate   19, 114, 150
anyone   31
anything   122, 140, 162, 169, 188, 226
appear   1
appetite   70
applicable   10, 51, 55, 147, 157, 176-177, 228, 249, 251
applied   33, 121, 163, 193, 202
appointed   34, 37
appraisal   16, 19, 33, 51, 54-55, 71-72, 87-88, 94, 102-103, 108, 112, 114, 116-117, 120-121, 123
appraisals   98, 105, 123
appraised   106, 111
appraiser   105, 116
appreciate   61
approach   31, 60, 65-67, 117, 122, 143, 221, 235-236, 243, 250
approaches   77, 198-199
approval   159, 215
approvals   142, 211
approve   67, 145, 150
approved   140, 145, 148, 184, 223-225
approving   148, 186
Architects   7
archived   184, 196
archives   260
arriving 142

articulate   235-236, 244
ascertain   66
ascribed   206
asking 1, 7, 190
aspects   106, 123, 210
assess 18, 96, 118, 123, 167, 223
assessed   19, 54, 200, 202
assessment   4-5, 8-9, 18, 62, 94, 98, 103, 138, 200, 204, 235, 237
assets 46, 255
assigned   23, 26, 141, 154, 156-157, 164, 210, 231, 239
Assignment   4, 192, 233
assist 8, 23, 71-72, 182, 201, 227
assistant   7
associated   17, 32, 57, 97, 116, 119
Assumption   3, 152
assurance   15, 25, 34, 54, 59-61, 63, 67-69, 77, 82, 85, 94, 98, 103, 107-109, 113-115, 119-120, 123-124, 127-128, 142, 178, 227, 264
assure 18, 41, 98
attain 126
attainable   34
attempted   31
attend 84, 213, 238
attendance   37
attendant   76
attended   37
attention   11
attitude   204, 260
attitudes   221
attribute   143
attributes   3, 24, 68, 93, 100, 113, 146, 163, 222-223
audience   113, 216
audited   261
auditing   87, 152
auditor 97, 249
auditors   249
audits 82, 116
augment   107
author 1, 145
authority   145, 194, 198, 200, 237, 258, 264
authorized   96, 156, 192, 246, 260
automated   81

automatic 261
automotive 85
available 30-31, 75, 79, 99, 161, 167, 176, 180-181, 200, 204-205, 208, 249
Average 11, 20, 37, 47, 64, 78, 90, 129, 252
avoided 84
background 9, 165
backing 137
backlog 113
backup 236
backward 225
balance 195
balanced 26, 115
balances 257
bandwidth 252
barriers 19, 198
baseline 4, 38, 67, 105, 159, 184, 196, 214
baselined 43, 159-160
basically 180
because 43
become 143-144, 148
becomes 227
before 9, 16, 31, 61-62, 103, 105, 161, 184, 201, 203, 223
beginning 2, 14, 20, 24, 37, 47, 64, 78, 91, 129
behave 23
behavior 260
behavioral 44
Behaviors 195, 227
behind 233
belief 10, 15, 21, 38, 48, 65, 79, 92
believe 43, 72, 110
benchmark 104, 122, 189
benchmarks 99
beneficial 86
benefit 1, 19, 56, 69, 74, 84, 89, 95, 111-112, 123, 160, 172
benefits 16, 39-40, 90, 92-93, 103-104, 106, 126, 138, 142, 146, 168, 238, 263
better 7, 32, 63, 70, 86, 107, 115, 117, 127, 174-175, 182, 214, 226-227, 232, 236, 253, 262
between 23, 45, 50, 71, 76, 94, 97-98, 108, 120-122, 124, 148, 157, 173, 179, 192, 198, 222, 243, 249, 255
beyond 18, 122, 244
bidder 258

bidding 181
biggest 219, 255
billed 258
bottleneck 175
boundaries 37, 233
bounds 37
Breakdown 3, 73, 154-155, 170
breaks 125
briefed 34
brings 33
broader 103
budget 73, 112, 141, 156, 161, 174, 176-177, 206, 210, 215, 249, 251, 254
Budgetary 257
budgeted 245
budgets 156-157, 193, 256
building 105, 108, 133, 247-248
builds 125
bundling 257
burdensome 63
burn-in 253
business 1, 7, 9, 34, 44, 51-52, 56, 60, 66, 88-89, 98, 106, 109, 114, 121, 133, 136, 145, 147, 156, 178-179, 185-186, 200, 204, 216, 224, 245, 249-250, 263
busywork 131
buy-in 115, 253
buyout 140
Calculate 165
calculated 246
called 241
cancel 113
canceled 113
cannot 168, 176
capability 40, 55, 61, 84, 125, 152, 184, 228, 264
capable 7, 28, 51
capacities 139
capacity 84, 138, 243
capture 43, 81, 85, 260
captured 196-197, 210, 215, 223
career 148
carried 208
categories 206, 236
caused 1

causes 41-42, 48, 80, 245
causing 44, 152, 245
celebrate 231
celebrated 236
center 56, 141
central 201
centrally 115
certain 66
certified 105, 123, 210
chains 55, 90
challenge 7, 226
challenges 42, 88, 90, 119, 237
champion 34
champions 191
chance 208
chances 204
change 5, 15, 30, 35, 42, 44, 49, 56, 61, 63, 68, 104, 111, 119, 125, 135, 144-145, 150-151, 163, 168, 176, 188, 197, 215-217, 222-225, 239, 258, 260-261, 264
changed 30, 34, 55, 182, 185, 218, 264
changes 21, 33-34, 36, 45, 53, 73, 76, 83, 86, 88, 102, 118, 126, 143, 145, 147, 150, 156-157, 172, 184, 192, 206, 210-211, 223-224, 235, 245, 261
changing 117, 136
channel 69, 77
channels 146, 204, 241
charges 258
charter 2, 29, 31, 133-134
charters 24
charts 43, 46
checked 81, 85, 89
checked-in 125
checking 257
checklists 8, 160
checks 55
choice 233
choose 10, 56, 120
chosen 241, 255, 257
circumvent 17
claimed 1
clarity 151
classes 211
classified 157

clearing 258
clearly 10, 15, 21, 38, 48, 65, 79, 92, 142, 146, 150, 159, 179, 195, 233, 258
client 35, 95, 253, 255
clients 35, 207, 228
climate 228-229
closed 87, 178, 196, 225, 260
closely 9, 176
Close-Out 6, 181, 260-262
Closing 6, 255
CMM-based 94
CMMI-ACQ 104
CMMI-dev 98, 107, 111
CMMI-SVC 19, 60, 96, 98, 103, 107, 116, 118, 120, 123
CMMI-x 117
coaches 26, 34, 190-191, 250
coding 153
co-exist 97, 105
cognitive 243
cognizant 236
coherent 159
collect 182, 190-191
collected 32, 38, 44, 69, 250
collection 39-40, 42-43, 46, 191
combine 108
combined 49, 95
combining 112, 123
command 101, 110
comments 253
commit 244
commitment 115, 245
committed 23, 30, 160, 197, 200, 205
Committee 152
common 41, 60, 62, 88, 97, 198, 212
community 62, 175, 182-183, 208, 229
companies 1, 73, 226
company 7
compare 82, 176, 247
compared 77, 159, 172, 196
comparing 157
comparison 10, 193, 212
compatible 42, 62, 97, 225
compelling 35

competency   105, 217
Competing   94, 118
competitor   245
compilers   249
complaints   228
complement   126
complete   1, 8, 10, 31, 36, 161, 163, 165, 174, 178, 189, 194, 233, 253, 261
completed   11, 23-24, 27-28, 61, 142, 161, 185, 200, 260
completely   174
completing   154
completion   22, 35, 143, 156, 167, 180, 231, 247, 262
complex   7, 217, 247
complexity   151, 179, 222
compliance   22, 41, 153, 249
compliant   52, 117
complied   232
comply   258
component   77, 97, 230
components   43, 46, 52-53, 143, 153
compute   11
computer   152, 257
concept   54, 150, 191
conception   77
concepts   51
Concern   194
concerns   17, 198, 251
concluded   77
conclusion   16, 102, 112
condition   85, 139
conditions   50, 81, 141, 184
conducive   228
conduct   86, 105, 123, 186
conducted   67, 76, 153, 178, 213, 223-224
conference   213
confidence   100, 206
confident   21-22, 167
confirm   10
conflict116, 127, 136, 144, 234
confronted   200
consensus   262
consider   17, 82, 125, 163, 172, 180, 257
considered   26, 92, 99, 212-214, 226

274

considers 187
consist 250
consistent 80, 139-140, 156, 228, 244
consortium 206
constant 74, 93, 113
constantly 239
Constraint 3, 152
consultant 7
consulted 198
consulting 100, 250
contact 7, 143
contain 87, 140, 237
contained 1
contains 8
content 29, 226
contents 1-2, 8
context 22, 28-31, 55
continual 83, 87
continue 60, 245
continuing 27
continuous 50, 99, 104, 124-125
contract 6, 156-157, 167-168, 180, 192, 210, 221, 231-232, 257-258, 260-261
contractor 5, 101, 106, 114, 127-128, 131, 150, 158, 180, 251, 257
contracts 178, 196, 251, 257, 260
contribute 77, 136, 138
control 2, 54, 73, 75, 79, 81, 84, 87, 140, 142, 144-145, 151, 156-157, 159, 183, 193, 214, 219, 222-223, 227, 238, 244
controlled 49, 202, 239
controls 82, 142, 167, 202, 249
convey 1
convince 192
cooperate 183
coordinate 59, 210
Copyright 1
corporate 229
correct 38, 42, 79, 90, 172, 176
corrected 178
correction 157
corrective 80, 196
correctly 23
correspond 8-9

countries 234
course 30, 247
coverage 116
covered 116, 120
covering 8, 194
crafted 49
crashing 168
create 54-55, 145
created 135, 139, 142, 160, 215
creating 7, 30, 152
creation 90
creativity 75
credible 183
criteria 2, 4, 8-9, 16, 31, 34, 39-40, 43, 45, 72, 99, 130, 148, 183, 185, 197, 212-213, 258, 260
CRITERION 2, 15, 21, 38, 48, 65, 79, 92
critical 25, 29, 32, 38, 40, 43, 86, 118, 165, 175, 206, 218, 227
criticism 235
criticized 236
cross-unit 51
crucial 218
crushed 93
crystal 10
Cultural 66, 137
culture 41, 93, 115, 119, 138, 194
cultures 234
current 24-25, 30, 33, 38, 45, 55, 66, 69, 113-114, 156, 167, 172, 194, 206, 211, 218-219, 222, 250, 255, 265
currently 30, 234, 237
curves 88
customer 18, 23, 25-26, 28, 32, 36, 41-42, 45, 80, 85, 88, 92, 102, 120, 124, 126, 146, 204, 217, 222, 231, 249, 254
customers 1, 19, 28-29, 37, 103, 152, 188, 204, 209, 221, 231, 245
customize 217
cut-down 247
damage 1
Dashboard 8
dashboards 86
day-to-day 83, 166
deadline 99, 258
debriefing 213
decide 66, 69, 74

decided 66, 231
decision 5, 180, 203, 212, 218, 226-227
decisions 69-70, 215, 226, 231-232
declare 51, 55
decline 47
decrease 188
dedicated 7
deeper 10
defect 22, 40, 189, 211
defects 32, 46, 62, 104, 172, 188-189, 229
define 2, 21, 24, 29, 58, 70, 79, 174, 180, 189, 207, 226
defined 10, 15, 21-22, 32-33, 37-38, 46, 48, 52-53, 55, 61, 65, 79, 89, 92, 132, 142, 151, 153-154, 159, 188, 194-195, 197, 233, 241
defining 7, 120, 134, 159
definite 87
definition 31, 74, 196, 204, 218, 257
degrading 44
degree 60, 235-238, 243-244
delayed 165
Delaying 236
delays 161, 174
delegate 234
delegated 28
deletions 86
deliver 16, 19, 25, 94, 174, 182, 231, 259
delivered 214-215, 232
delivering 61, 237
delivers 170
delivery 69, 104, 125, 165, 167, 216, 261, 263
demand 111
demands 47, 243
demoted 96
department 7, 143, 220
depend 221
dependent 256
depending 29
deployed 80
derive 100
derived 42, 45, 51
describe 35, 40, 76, 102, 112, 118, 133, 143-144, 148, 166, 180, 215, 251, 262
described 1, 57, 147, 184, 224

describes 173
describing 27, 173
deserve 262
deserving 220
design 1, 9, 21, 34, 39-40, 47, 73, 75-76, 97, 138, 145, 152, 205, 215
designated 160
designed 7, 9, 62, 66, 77, 93
designing 7
designs 67
desired 30, 170-171, 224, 247, 255
despite 57
detail 63, 133, 155, 257
detailed 143, 157, 161, 179
details 217
detect 81
detection 249
determine 9, 23, 27, 31, 34, 58, 74, 102, 113, 161, 172-173, 182, 196, 213, 234, 262
determined 190-191, 258
determines 136, 180
develop 57, 65-66, 70, 86, 140, 144, 155, 215, 244
developed 9, 24, 29, 32, 66, 71-72, 75, 77, 142, 144, 173, 191, 224, 247-248
developer 70, 74, 77
developers 59, 71, 145, 222
developing 88, 212, 238
deviation 173
device 85, 119, 228-230
DevOps 93
diagnostic 208
diagram 3, 167-168, 176
diagrams 106
Dictionary 3, 156
difference 50, 98, 122, 227
different 7, 23, 29, 36, 53, 62, 65, 67, 72, 93, 122, 128, 206, 226, 257, 262
difficult 162, 170, 172, 184
difficulty 207, 218
direct 156, 246
direction 30
directions 208
directly 1, 56

Directory	5, 231
Disagree	10, 15, 21, 38, 48, 65, 79, 92
disasters	95
discipline	71
disclosed	212
disclosure	157
discord	108
discovered	34, 67, 77
dispersion	107
display	46
displayed	32, 43-44, 174
disposed	184
disputes	260
distribute	215, 231
divergent	139
Divided	20, 28, 37, 47, 63, 78, 90, 129
division	141
document	9, 36, 59, 68, 82, 140, 145-147, 227, 255
documented	29, 52, 60, 67-68, 79, 82-83, 89-90, 132, 142, 144, 150, 152-153, 184, 195, 210, 241, 249, 254
documents	7, 67, 151, 156, 196, 238
dollars	246
domain	29
dominant	51
drawback	215
drawings	230
drivers	44
duplicate	25
duplicates	144
duration	3, 46, 114, 120, 138-139, 154, 167, 172-174, 200, 205
durations	33, 176
during	30, 34, 54, 56, 71, 74-75, 117, 121, 131, 160, 163, 169, 179, 189, 196, 200, 245
duties	60, 257
dynamics	24
earlier	62
earliest	144
earned	5, 247
easier	50
economic	208, 258, 264
economy	172, 219
eDiscovery	227

edition 8
editorial 1
education 82, 103, 217
effect 72, 255
effective 42, 53, 73, 84, 86, 123-124, 127, 152, 174, 208, 213, 226, 228-229, 250, 257, 264
effects 138, 165, 236
efficiency 73, 102
efficient 86, 122, 139, 221, 257, 264
effort 32, 66, 73, 76, 86, 128, 140, 143, 156-157, 192, 217
efforts 31, 50, 76, 81, 88, 256
either 33, 163, 236
electronic 1, 33, 101
element 35, 107
elements 9, 61, 133, 150, 156, 159, 190, 192, 218
elicit 190
eliminate 177, 208
e-mail 146
embarking 35
embedded 85
emerging 85, 238
emphasis 226
emphasize 67
empirical 249
employed 152
employee 237, 251
employees 180, 229, 237-238, 249
employers 135
empower 7
enabling 229
encourage 75, 103
end-users 200
energy 125
engage 233, 236, 239, 243
engagement 135, 199, 210, 229, 233, 239
engineers 102
enhance 111
enough 7, 49, 85, 100, 111, 145-146, 148, 235
ensure 27, 33, 42, 76, 79, 82, 138-139, 142, 186, 194, 233, 242, 244, 257
ensuring 9, 229, 247-248
Enterprise 45, 89, 124, 220
entities 140

entitled 213
entity 1
equipment 21
equipped 31
equitably 28, 244
equivalent 258
errors 62, 157, 249
escalated 242
escalation 61, 185, 265
especially 26, 172
essential 19, 83, 101, 244
essentials 216
establish 25, 49, 65, 112, 114, 126, 183
estimate 104, 128, 141, 159, 172, 174, 212, 253
-estimate 180
estimated 22, 29, 35, 182-183, 212, 251
estimates 3-4, 33, 141, 156, 172, 180, 215
estimating 3-4, 143, 174, 182, 210, 214
estimation 139, 172
ethical 229, 253
ethics 204
evaluate 62, 66, 150, 192, 214, 218, 257
evaluated 60, 68, 184, 228
evaluating 71-72, 75
evaluation 39, 65, 189, 212-213, 258
evaluators 212
events 19, 133, 172-173
eventual 16
everyone 27-28, 52, 58, 188
everything 226
evidence 10, 26, 98, 111, 114, 221, 258
evolution 38
exactly 50, 189
examined 257
examining 77
Example 2, 8, 12, 157, 249, 257
examples 7-8, 24, 133
exceed 42, 154, 167
exceeding 194
excellence 7, 56
excelling 194
except 94, 109, 157
excessive 73

exchange 243
exciting 237
exclude 107, 112
excluded 45
exclusive 87
execute 43, 49, 55, 59
executed 42-43, 225
Executing 5, 198, 218
execution 140, 152, 196
executive 7
Exercise 167
exercises 235
existence 204
existing 9, 42, 81, 112, 127, 141, 150, 173
exists 70, 167
expect 80, 98, 102-103, 109, 112, 119, 126, 141, 207, 263
expected 16, 24, 33, 76, 99, 112, 114, 120, 127, 172, 180, 226, 241, 263
expecting 262
expense 156
expensive 35
experience 58, 88, 115, 125, 140, 165, 204, 206, 251
expertise 140-141, 179
experts 29, 258
expiration 168
explained 9
explicit 53, 228
explore 238
explored 187
export 128
extent 10, 37, 107-108, 138-139
external 31, 45, 101, 197, 228, 257
facilitate 10, 44, 86, 95, 98
facilities 39, 112, 146, 213, 228
facing 17
factor 145
factors 18, 38, 40, 49, 83, 87, 108, 116, 168, 182
factory 103
failed 77
failing 202
failure 36, 228
failures 86
fairly 28

falling 62
familiar 8
families 180
fashion 1, 23
faster 74
faults 100
favorable   245
feasible   159, 183, 203
feature 9
features   96, 99, 118, 126-127, 140, 254
federal 35
feedback   25, 32
figure 40
filling 43
finalize 67, 181
finalized   12
finally 145
financial   107, 136-138, 249
findings   51, 55, 189
fingertips   9
finish   144, 161, 163, 165, 167, 247-248
finishing   53
Fiscal 88, 250
fitness 29
focused   196
follow 90, 215, 241, 253
followed   24, 61, 71, 75, 153, 201, 210, 214-215, 223
following   8, 10, 60, 83, 88, 186
follow-on   255
forces 188
forecast   178, 248
Forecasts   178
forget 9
formal 6, 24, 33, 61, 67, 71, 145, 153, 157, 160, 196, 214, 223, 243-244, 253-254
formally   246
format 9, 231
formed 23, 26
formula   11
Formulate   21
forward   109, 111
forwarded   192
foster 194

frames 257
framework 85, 90, 106, 111, 123, 190
frameworks 60
frequency 87, 191
frequent 125, 150, 160
frequently 117, 235, 238
friends 180, 236
fulfill 29
full-scale 75
fulltime 160, 197
function 44, 69, 77, 150, 254, 262
functional 97, 156-157
functions 51, 170, 194, 204
funded 159
funding 202, 256
further 203
future 7, 20, 44, 85, 101, 138, 141, 206, 245
gained 81, 87
gather 10, 38, 98
gathered 144
gathering 147, 214
general 103, 163, 211, 253
generally 221
generate 67, 188
generated 72, 156
generation 8, 264
generators 249
generic 57, 119
geographic 233
getting 114, 198, 227
glaring 16
govern 243
governance 60, 124, 138, 142, 152, 210
government 106, 172
granted 184
graphs 8, 43
greater 138
grievance 229
ground 47
grouping 257
groups 57, 127, 142, 178, 210, 216, 220, 229, 243
growing 47, 172
growth 92, 166, 264

guaranteed 27
guidance 1
guidelines 227
guides 140
guiding 110
handle 169
handled 157, 233
handling 207
happen 15, 127, 165, 203, 208
happened 23
happens 7, 74, 125, 182, 208-209, 261
hardly 247
hardware 103, 152, 173
harmonized 50
harness 93
Havent 201
having 143, 245
hazards 208
health 44
helpdesk 222
helpful 39, 63, 102
helping 7, 139, 218
higher 68, 70, 114, 189
highest 125
high-level 23, 28, 133, 147
highlight 194
hinder 194
hiring 86
historical 182
history 128, 161, 264
hitting 247
hot-fix 53
humans 7
hypotheses 48
identified 1, 17-18, 28, 36-38, 41, 45-46, 146, 150, 156, 164, 178-179, 184, 189, 195, 209, 215, 217, 227, 246, 257
identifier 133
identify 9-10, 16, 62-63, 67, 152, 182, 192-193, 245, 249, 258
ideology 264
imbedded 87
Immediate 47, 136
impact 4, 33, 37, 39-40, 43, 45-47, 67, 131, 138, 184, 200, 202, 204-206, 216, 224, 235, 242, 255, 265

impacted	103, 142, 150, 196
impacting	44
impacts	138, 142, 174, 200, 263
implement	17, 25-27, 30, 42, 46, 49, 59, 79, 107, 111, 145
implements	27
implicit	228
importance	56, 238, 244
important	18, 55, 58, 72, 121, 134, 145, 170, 199, 212, 237, 239, 241
imprecise	97
improper	229
improve	2, 9, 52, 54, 56-57, 61-62, 65, 68-70, 73-75, 77, 170, 188-189, 232, 262-263
improved	59, 71, 78, 84-85, 138
improving	53, 68, 73, 221, 249
inaccurate	145
incentives	86, 93, 259
include	59, 107, 112, 116, 144, 178, 197, 213
included	2, 7, 45, 54, 100, 103-104, 112-113, 138, 173-174, 183, 222, 251, 260
includes	9, 42, 216
including	27, 31, 34, 73, 112, 156, 215, 258
incomplete	145
increase	63, 246
increased	250
increasing	226
indeed	17
in-depth	8, 10
indicate	33, 45, 85
indicated	80, 257
indirect	156-157, 180, 192-193
indirectly	1
individual	1, 39, 84, 122-123, 161, 186, 193, 243, 251, 262
induction	86
industrial	75
industry	85, 97, 101-102, 166, 196, 211, 229
industrys	115
influence	83, 115, 135, 194, 226, 239, 258, 262
influences	199
inform	235
informed	114, 131
ingrained	88
inherent	194

inhibit   18, 66
in-house   133, 186
initial   70, 126, 176, 187
initiated   182, 188, 225
Initiating   2, 131
initiative   10, 32, 133, 186, 190-191, 239
Innovate   65
innovation   101, 105, 186, 258
innovative   174, 182, 219
inputs   23, 27, 80
insights 8
inspect 84
inspection   61
Institute   105
instructed   145
intangible   39, 45
integrate   104, 125, 140
Integrated   184
integrity   123, 224
intended   1, 72
INTENT 15, 21, 38, 48, 65, 79, 92
intention   1
intentions   228
interact   110, 122
interest 127, 220
interested   32, 84, 258, 263
interests   16, 216, 258
interface   101, 110
internal   1, 31, 52, 156-157, 192, 249
interpret   10, 31
introduced   150, 243
invalid 117
inventory   180-181
invest   109
invested   69
investment   55, 69, 105, 116, 190
invitee 142
invoice 232
invoices   257
involved   19, 26, 53, 56, 66, 73, 89, 98, 116, 122, 136, 142-143, 159, 178, 193, 204, 214, 218, 221, 257, 260, 263
involves   145
involving   228

isolate 245
issues 20, 67, 131, 147, 150, 152-153, 160, 167, 169, 242, 263, 265
itself 1, 17, 56
joining 150
judgment 1
keeping 30
knowing 258
knowledge 9, 31, 81, 84, 86-87, 185-186, 194, 216-217, 261
labeled 193
labeling 228
landscape 51
language 102
larger 76
latest 8
launch 32, 52
laundry 144
leader 34, 127, 206
leaders 26-27, 77, 199, 250
leadership 29
leanest 96
learned 6, 80, 85-86, 88, 178, 253, 255, 262, 264
learning 80, 84, 88, 226
leaves 103
lesson 255, 262
lessons 6, 75, 80, 85-86, 126, 178, 253, 262, 264-265
letter 146
Leveling 164
levels 18, 29, 44, 72, 85, 100, 103-104, 121-122, 125, 154, 206
leverage 28, 85, 104-105, 109, 175, 182, 233
leveraged 31
leveraging 238
levers 54, 217
liability 1
libraries 99
licensed 1
lifecycle 29, 55, 82, 120
life-cycle 71
Lifetime 9
likelihood 138, 201-202, 204
likely 185, 206, 226, 245
limitation 106, 124
limited 9, 194

linked 24, 147, 227
linking 23
listed 1, 58, 190
listen 233
literature 18
little 110, 144
locally 115
located 56
lock-in 84, 86
logged 21, 222
logical 156, 168-169
logically 159
logistics 94
longer 19
long-term 76, 81
looking 118
machine 80, 103
maintain 49, 79, 112, 128
maintained 51, 81, 230
makers 180
making 139, 143, 190, 203, 218
manage 32, 54, 99, 116, 131, 134, 140, 144, 148, 159, 166, 177, 180, 185-186, 214, 231, 245
manageable 29, 96, 143
managed 7, 99, 114, 265
management 1, 3-5, 8-9, 16, 18, 26, 28-31, 33-34, 46, 54, 56-57, 60, 69, 73, 77, 80, 82, 88, 94, 97, 99, 107, 109, 113, 115, 121, 125-126, 128, 132, 136, 140-142, 144, 150, 153, 159-160, 172-173, 176, 178, 180, 186-187, 189, 192, 195-200, 202, 206, 210, 213-214, 216, 218-221, 229, 241, 245-247, 249, 253-254, 257, 260
manager 7, 9, 22, 27, 86, 107, 118, 181, 210, 220, 253
managers 2, 54, 57, 130, 196
manages 121, 251
managing 2, 22-23, 118, 123, 127, 130, 135, 145, 263
mandate 137
mandatory 224, 262
manifesto 108
manner 152, 156, 253
mapped 26
mapping 75, 218
margin 159
marked 16
market 166, 172, 203, 219, 236, 245, 247, 258

marketable 203
marketer 7
marketing 146, 153, 262
master 156
material 107, 165, 189, 213, 245-246
materials 1, 229
matrices 148
Matrix 2-4, 136, 148-149, 192, 206, 218
matter 29, 51
matters 93
maturing 107
maturity 18, 29, 46, 49, 51, 55-56, 58, 65-66, 69-70, 89-90, 92-93, 97-98, 100-106, 109, 114, 117-118, 121-122, 125-127
maximize 238
meaning 163, 233
meaningful 237
measurable 23, 34, 180, 244
measure 2, 9, 19, 28, 31, 38-45, 52, 57, 65, 69, 133, 136-137, 182-183, 191, 218
measured 39, 45-46, 80, 157, 188, 209, 235
measures 38-39, 41-42, 44-46, 57, 85, 208, 219, 249
mechanical 1
mechanism 34, 263
mechanisms 71, 75, 137, 139
mechanized 211
medical 85, 101, 119
medium 49, 247
meeting 21, 25, 36, 51, 85-86, 142, 179, 191, 194, 196, 210, 221, 226, 228, 231, 233-234, 239-240, 249
meetings 26-27, 36-37, 109, 142, 180, 211, 227
Member 5, 29, 117, 170, 199, 220, 237
members 23, 27-28, 30, 33-34, 36, 66, 73, 86, 114, 143-144, 150, 159-160, 176, 178, 197, 214, 231-238, 243-244, 250
membership 236, 243-244
memorable 188, 237
Mentally 145
message 216
messages 111, 234, 239
method 62, 94, 109, 140, 175, 178, 187, 198, 216, 223, 235-236
methods 25, 35, 45, 59, 71, 75, 97, 112, 121, 183, 204, 212, 234
metrics 4, 40, 50, 55, 65, 71, 77, 86, 93, 97, 144, 152, 188, 214

milestone   3, 128, 133, 159, 165, 167, 196, 210
milestones   31-32, 135, 163, 179
minimize   138, 255
minimum   252
minutes   36, 196, 210, 231, 234
missing 117, 164
Mission 137, 208
Mitigate   138
mitigation   140, 177
mobilized   138
models 49, 53, 55, 76-77, 89-90, 94, 102, 106, 114, 121, 124-125, 127-128
modern   121, 173
modified   78, 88, 223
modules   17, 99
moments   215
monitor   72, 80, 89, 137, 182, 242
monitored   161, 174
monitoring   5, 80-81, 83-84, 145, 169, 241, 250, 257
motivated   95
motivation   70
motive 190
moving   68, 104-105, 114
multiple   86, 200, 206
mutually   87, 112
narrative   153
national   138, 208, 218, 234
nature 29, 245
nearest   11
necessary   43, 48, 66, 72, 104, 128, 138-139, 142, 158, 182, 193, 206, 217, 225, 241, 243
needed   17-18, 23, 55, 59, 80, 88, 133, 178-182, 190, 196, 264
needle 42
negative   216
negatively   102, 109, 196, 203, 218
negotiated   217
neither 1
nervous   145
network   3, 102, 167-168, 176, 243-244
networks   173
Neutral 10, 15, 21, 38, 48, 65, 79, 92
normal 88, 157

normally 82
noteworthy 77
nothing 100
notice 1, 215
noticed 83
noticing 227
notified 198, 212, 261
noting 223
number 20, 32, 37, 47, 63, 78, 90, 129, 163, 189, 234, 257-258, 266
numerous 260-261
objective 7, 54, 136, 138, 184, 201, 206, 218, 227
objectives 18, 21, 24, 94, 99, 142, 178-179, 185-186, 196, 198, 202-203, 221, 231, 244
objects 51
observable 49
observe 195
observed 69
observing 152
obstacles 17, 88, 96, 166, 174, 182
obtain 22, 263
obtained 32, 142
obviously 10
occurred 187
occurring 71, 204-205
occurs 105, 131, 205, 255
offers 73, 212, 258
office 97, 99, 220, 261
officials 260
offshore 68, 147
one-time 7
ongoing 44, 80, 161, 174, 249
operate 208, 233
operates 101
operating 5, 80, 100, 139, 192, 233
operation 82, 174
operations 9, 86, 88, 103, 185
operators 90, 188, 258
opinion 228
opponent 226
opponents 199
opposed 239
optimal 71, 74, 121, 252

optimally 228
optimize 69, 75
organized 82
orient 85
oriented 160
origin 146
original 156, 177, 200, 227
originate 198
others 79, 94, 97, 116, 131, 144, 182-183, 185, 187-188, 194, 198-199, 203, 206-207, 226, 244, 262
otherwise 1, 66, 157, 184, 258
outcome 10, 45, 170-171
outcomes 72, 97, 99, 116, 137, 174, 182, 229, 242, 247, 249, 255, 262
outlier 164
output 28, 46, 81, 85
outputs 27, 80, 169, 215
outside 75, 180
Outsource 110, 260
overall 9-10, 18, 46, 51, 167, 227, 241, 251
overcome 174, 182
overhead 54, 156-157, 192-193, 245-246
overlap 107
overlook 239
overlooked 219, 265
overruns 192
oversight 150
overtime 163
over-time 55
owners 59, 154
ownership 46, 81
package 126, 157
packages 47, 157
packaging 228
parallel 67, 81, 167
parameter 29
parameters 43, 86
partial 53
particular 39, 59, 63, 74, 105-106, 109, 125, 258
Parties 258, 260
partner 119
partners 19, 71, 138-139, 263
passed 94

patches   61
pattern   163
patterns   45
payment   211, 257, 260
payments   210
pending   225
people 7, 51, 56, 58, 61, 105, 110, 136, 152, 173, 191-193, 200, 206, 208, 220, 247
percentage 148
perform   23, 25, 28, 54, 79, 83, 144, 152, 170, 236, 253, 257
performant 49
performed   24, 92-93, 148, 161-162, 201, 231, 237
performing 17, 83, 89
perhaps   76, 247
period 65
periodic   94, 127
permission 1
permit 158
persist 42
person 1, 137, 143, 198
personally 148
personnel   42, 114, 168, 176, 179, 190-191
phased   67
phases 62, 76, 82, 163, 200
phasing   112
phrase 145
physical   33
pilots   67
pitfalls 42, 62
planned   42-43, 81, 145, 157, 162, 172, 214, 262-263
planning   3, 8, 82-88, 131, 138, 140, 144, 169, 220, 228-229
pocket 175
pockets   175
points 20, 37, 47, 63, 78, 90, 129, 191
policies   140
policy 79, 82, 142, 152, 169, 210, 229, 250, 265
political   66, 165, 239, 264
portfolio   97, 126, 241
portfolios 239
position   194, 250
positioned 49, 182-183
positions   250
positive   121, 216, 228-229

positively   196, 203
possess 243
possible   53, 67, 72, 79, 86, 96, 104, 108, 174, 211, 228-229, 243, 258
potential   40, 66, 71-72, 88, 146, 173, 192-193, 198, 208, 241
practical   63, 65, 79, 220
practice   97, 111, 114-116, 206
practices   1, 9, 33, 42, 56-57, 63, 68, 75, 83, 85-86, 89, 95, 104, 115, 119, 122, 140, 152, 160, 194, 237, 254
precaution   1
precise 258
predict 100, 222
prediction   163
predictive   170
prefer 125
preferred   216, 263
pre-filled   8
prepare   190, 212, 239
prepared   106, 213
preparing   235, 262
present   44, 85, 109, 145, 216, 219, 249
presented   61, 223, 231
presenting   234
preserve   37
pressing   131
pressured   107
prevent   62, 87, 172, 212
prevented   19
preventive   208
previous   31, 176-177, 189, 251, 255
previously   225
priced 156
prices 212
primarily   196
primary   95, 172, 245
principal   121
principle   217
principles   67, 85, 100-101
priorities   115, 216
prioritize   36
priority 164, 238, 244
private 138

problem 15, 18, 21, 31, 34, 36, 61, 63, 66, 172, 220, 227, 247
problems 16-17, 41, 57, 61-62, 71, 80, 110, 190
procedure 50, 58, 68, 229, 233, 250, 257-258
procedures 9, 80, 82-83, 90, 158-160, 169, 181, 186-187, 190, 210, 215, 223, 227, 257-258
proceed 192, 246
proceeding 176
process 1-7, 9, 23-24, 27-28, 32, 36, 39-41, 43-44, 46, 48-63, 69, 71-73, 78-79, 81-90, 95-96, 101, 110, 131, 138, 143-145, 147-148, 151-152, 159, 169, 172-173, 175-176, 190-191, 195-196, 200-202, 206, 214-215, 218, 226, 229, 231-232, 241, 247-249, 251, 254-255, 257-258, 263-264
processed 257
processes 26, 49, 51-54, 57-59, 61, 83, 85-86, 88, 99, 112, 132, 137, 150, 153, 173, 186, 215, 222, 224, 241, 245, 254-255
produce 107, 133, 138, 169, 221, 232, 241
produced 138, 214
producing 116, 148
product 1, 15, 22-24, 30, 50, 54-55, 59, 62-63, 69-70, 103, 118, 122, 127, 136, 145, 150, 166, 184, 186, 189, 200, 203-204, 220-221, 225, 232, 247-249, 254-255
production 35, 94, 109, 153
products 1, 29, 44, 51, 58, 70, 94, 96, 99, 113, 118, 136, 139, 148, 219, 221, 224
profile 228
profit 188
program 18-19, 25, 35, 52, 67, 71, 127, 138-139, 194, 218-219, 230, 242
programme 138, 242
programs 49, 54, 62, 94, 109, 123, 138, 140, 220, 239, 257
progress 34, 133, 139, 152, 182, 190, 211, 214, 218-219, 242
prohibited 157
project 2-8, 16, 18, 24-26, 28-30, 33-35, 44-46, 50, 56, 58, 63, 66, 69, 73-74, 77, 79-80, 82-83, 86, 88-89, 93, 95, 97, 99-100, 104, 106-107, 113-114, 116, 118, 120-122, 126, 128, 130-140, 142-148, 150-152, 154, 157, 159-162, 165-168, 170-186, 195-198, 200, 202-205, 210-211, 214-215, 217-222, 224-225, 231-232, 235, 241, 243, 247, 251, 253-256, 260, 262-265
projects 2, 19, 49, 93-94, 99, 107, 112-113, 115, 118, 128, 130, 139-140, 148, 151, 196, 200-201, 204, 206, 221, 231, 233, 239, 247, 256
promise 124

promote 136, 186
promoted 35
promptly 235, 242
proofing 69
proper 211
properly 27, 131, 146, 157, 222, 258-259
properties 119
proponents 199
Proposal 212, 255
proposals 212, 218
proposed 53, 66, 72, 88-89, 100, 102, 123, 137, 140, 146, 251-252
proved 254
proven 101
provide 27, 39, 53, 77, 94, 125, 135, 156-157, 167, 172, 174, 180, 182, 188, 243
provided 11, 57, 90, 96, 136, 160, 178, 186, 217
provider 19, 68, 101
providers 39, 68, 102
provides 146
providing 133, 135
provision 197, 226
public 138, 210
publicly 99
publisher 1
purchase 7, 25
purchases 215
purchasing 257
purpose 2, 9, 29, 39, 182, 190, 222, 226, 236-238
purposes 95, 124
qualified 28, 123, 178
quality 1, 4-5, 9, 15-16, 18, 22, 24-25, 29-30, 33, 38-44, 46-47, 60-63, 65, 67-77, 80-87, 93-94, 96-104, 107-111, 113-115, 117-128, 139, 142, 159, 173, 178, 184, 186-188, 191, 214, 222, 227-230, 232, 249, 264
quantities 213
quantity 111, 259
quarterly 65
quarters 245
question 10, 15, 21, 38, 48, 65, 79, 92, 190
questions 7-8, 10, 60, 100, 174
quickly 9, 181
Random 41

rapidly 47
raters 238
rather 72
rating 108
ratings 94, 119, 213
rational 156, 245
rationale 179, 227
reached 125
readiness 69, 75
readings 89
realistic 116, 141, 177, 219, 244, 249
realize 106, 127
really 7, 95, 100, 121-122, 145
reasonable 96, 141, 153, 159, 215, 258
reasons 35, 120, 211
reassess 197
re-assign 163
receive 8-9, 22, 216, 239
received 34, 117, 211, 235
receivers 217
receiving 229
receptive 258
recipient 261
RECOGNIZE 2, 15
recognized 211, 240, 243
recommend 94
record 23, 63, 101, 190
recorded 178, 246
recording 1, 186, 223, 233
records 70, 128, 187, 260
recovered 95
recovery 36
recruiting 229
recurrence 208
recurring 158
redesign 54
reduce 25, 43, 139, 192
reduced 45, 208
reducing 85
reference 53
references 258, 266
reflect 90, 152, 262
reflected 89

reform 139
regard 16, 87-88, 114, 117, 120-121, 139
regarding   152, 181, 221
Register   2, 4, 135, 144, 202
regular 34, 36, 150, 249, 251
regularly   27, 36-37, 180
regulation   206, 238
regulator   92
regulators   98, 103
regulatory   214
reinforced   139
reject 150
rejected   223
relate 101, 224
related 60, 65, 89, 95, 184, 193, 222, 239, 247, 264
relates 23
relation   71, 113
relative 212, 238, 244
release 27, 96, 98, 153, 178, 189, 196
releases   74, 251
releasing   61
relevant   34, 100, 143, 184, 243
reliable 31, 95, 116, 208
reliably 235
relocation   140
relying 236
remain 265
remaining   176, 182, 263
remedies   47
remember   175
remove   67, 208
rendered   101
repair 211
repeated   74
rephrased   9
replace   87, 255
replanning   156
report 5, 89, 113, 214, 220, 232, 243, 251, 262, 264
reported   150, 196, 239, 247
reporting   15, 18, 40, 65, 69, 77, 80, 99, 156, 223
reports 114, 126, 128, 135, 160, 172, 181, 192, 211, 214, 249
repository   196
represent   44, 224-225

reproduced 1
request 5, 197, 212, 222-225
requested 1, 223-224
requests 22, 27, 104, 222, 258
require 33, 169, 215, 238
required 25, 30-33, 35, 40, 42, 136, 156, 161, 167, 174, 203-204, 211, 233, 258, 263-265
requires 30
requiring 135, 261
research 229, 238
reserved 1
reserves 215
reside 234
resistance 216
resolution 61
resolve 163, 234
resolved 16, 242, 265
resource 3-4, 27, 115, 139, 145, 156, 160, 163-164, 169-170, 172, 196, 219-220
resources 2, 7, 29-31, 55, 73, 111-112, 136, 138, 141, 147, 151, 159, 161, 163-164, 167-168, 170, 175-176, 178, 182, 186, 214, 217, 231, 242-243
respect 1, 23
respond 202
responded 11
response 80, 85, 87, 252
responses 99, 203
responsive 183
restricted 258
result 53, 62, 74, 150, 182, 196, 198, 224, 260, 263
resulted 83, 237
resulting 138, 156
results 8, 25, 33, 50-51, 65, 74, 77, 89-90, 138-139, 172, 176, 178, 182, 189, 218, 237, 241-242, 253
Retain 92
return 116, 168, 190
revenue 250
review 9, 23, 25-27, 57-58, 95, 117, 128, 141, 168, 176, 185, 215, 223
reviewed 32, 94, 127, 150, 187-188, 228
reviewer 236
reviewers 235
reviewing 56

reviews 70, 88, 113, 153, 178, 211-212, 249
revised 83
revisions 261
revisit 227
Reward 220
rewards 86
reworking 41
rights 1, 113
robust 60, 82
routine 89
running 125
rushing 239
safety 21-22, 30, 54, 97
satisfied 127, 253-255
satisfies 248
satisfy 114, 131
savings 33
Scaled 90
SCAMPI 16, 87-88, 93, 102, 105, 112, 114, 116-117, 120-121, 123
scenario 173, 219
schedule 3-4, 30, 73, 112, 126, 144, 156, 159, 167, 176-177, 184, 193, 197, 206, 214, 219, 224, 231, 245, 251
scheduled 144, 179-180, 211, 245
schedules 16, 156, 168
scheduling 143, 211
scheme 87
Science 175
scientific 175
Scorecard 2, 11-13
scorecards 86
Scores 13
scoring 9
screen 222, 233
scripts 153
scrumming 108
second 11
section 11, 20, 37, 47, 63-64, 78, 90, 129
sector 15, 247
secure 54
secured 70
security 22, 26, 35, 54, 93, 99, 116, 123, 135, 152, 201, 224
segmented 36

segments 29
select 76, 258
selected 71, 76, 182-183, 237
selecting 233
selection 4, 212, 215, 218, 235
sellers 1
selling 226
senders 217
senior 94, 172
separate 50, 55, 69, 77, 257
separated 157
sequence 39, 106, 156, 162, 168
sequencing 196
series 10
serious 145
service 1-2, 7, 15, 18, 41, 45, 73, 80, 84, 95-96, 119, 124, 150, 166, 186, 203, 220-221
services 1, 17, 94-95, 98, 101, 111, 113, 120, 136, 202, 228, 251-253, 261
serving 97
session 144
settings 116
shared 81, 182, 226
sharing 186, 233, 244
shorten 173
should 7, 15, 28, 36, 46, 51, 59, 65, 71, 73, 77-78, 85-86, 89, 93, 96, 99, 103-108, 113-114, 118, 131, 135, 138, 140, 143-144, 157, 161, 163, 170, 174, 178, 180, 187-188, 190, 194, 202, 205, 207-208, 212-213, 216-217, 222, 224, 231, 238, 241, 246, 255, 262
-should 185
signatures 169
signed 150
signers 260
similar 24, 31, 83, 161, 189, 204
simple 244, 247
simply 8, 250
simulator 235
single 117
single-use 7
situation 18, 38, 127, 218, 247
skills 42, 118, 131-132, 165, 181, 196, 200, 217-218, 236, 243-244, 257
smooth 265

social   19, 137, 208, 228, 250, 264
software   15-16, 18, 22-23, 25, 29-30, 33-34, 38-44, 46-47, 49, 52-53, 58-63, 65-72, 74-75, 77, 80-82, 84-86, 93-94, 96-99, 101-103, 105-110, 113-120, 123-124, 126-128, 147, 173, 200-201, 222, 230, 251
solicit   25
soliciting   234
solution   65-68, 71-76, 79, 122, 153, 251-252
solutions   66-67, 72, 76, 88, 140, 202, 264
solving 66
Someone   7
someones   236
something   34, 120, 143
source 4, 17, 31, 208, 212, 218
sources   67, 147, 207
special 17, 41, 90, 216
specific   8, 17, 23, 34, 57, 74, 93, 142, 150, 152, 162, 169-170, 172, 184, 195-196, 218, 220, 224, 229, 262
specified   156, 258-259
spending   40, 93, 113
sponsor   18, 133, 150, 178-179, 217, 254, 262
sponsored   34
sponsors   19, 180, 191, 231
spread 83, 90
sprint   34, 82, 86, 113
stability 41, 55
stable   24, 200
staffed 30
staffing 34, 86, 228
staged 99, 124
stages   34, 140, 197, 257
standard   7, 83, 88-90, 169, 173, 251
standards   1, 9-10, 82, 84-86, 88, 142, 157, 186, 189, 191, 212, 224, 258
started 8
starting 9
stated   42, 76, 146, 193, 258
Statement   3, 10, 112, 142, 145, 150-151, 157, 197, 210
statements   11, 20, 31, 34, 37, 47, 63, 78, 90, 97, 129, 190
status   5, 56, 88, 102, 113-114, 128, 131, 145, 150, 160, 196, 211, 214, 220, 222, 232, 247, 251
statute 238
Steering   152

strategic   87, 106, 127, 133, 178, 186, 228
strategies   118, 123, 127, 177, 217, 226, 249
strategy   18, 70, 74, 90, 104, 108, 138, 159, 218, 227
strengthen   83
strengths   165, 184, 254
Strongly   10, 15, 21, 38, 48, 65, 79, 92
structural   235
structure   3, 73, 99, 105, 121, 124, 151, 154-155, 170, 244
structured   31, 143
structures   42, 138, 192
studies 18, 95
subdivide   156
subject8-9, 29
subjected   73
submit 35
submitted   224
sub-teams   243
succeed   235
success   17-19, 31, 38, 40, 50, 100, 121, 168, 186, 197, 206, 215, 219, 221, 226, 241, 244, 255
successes   86
successful   35, 76, 82, 198, 221
suffered   235
sufficient   25, 68, 114, 138-139
suggest   223, 228
suggested   80, 224-225
suitable   43, 63, 249, 258
summarize   258
summary   172, 192
sunsetting   110
supervisor   237
supplier   25, 53, 121, 257
suppliers   27, 59, 116
supplies   253, 257
support   7, 33, 49, 53, 69, 72, 82, 88, 97, 106, 110, 127, 136, 169, 186, 211, 237, 252
supported   23, 128, 146, 218
supporting   66, 160
supports   50, 101
surface   80
SUSTAIN   2, 55, 92
sustained   110
sustaining   81

sw-CMM 97, 110
symptom 15
symptoms 109
synergies 136
system 9, 34, 36, 61, 68, 70-71, 75, 81, 84, 86, 93, 97, 102, 110, 113, 116, 119-121, 123, 126-128, 146-147, 152, 157, 170, 195, 200, 211, 224, 229, 247-248, 258
systems 42, 83, 86, 112, 137, 157, 211, 216, 229, 247, 249, 254
tactics 226
tailored 213
taking 72, 221, 234
talents 196
talking 7
tangible 40, 43
target 36, 105, 113, 188, 210, 216
targeted 67
targets 133, 180, 247
tasked 81
taxation 249
teamed 234
technical 66, 100, 110, 132, 136, 141, 147, 206, 212-213, 223, 264
techniques 26, 30, 36, 46, 121, 159, 215
technology 81, 114, 166, 172, 202, 206-207, 233-234
template 43, 176-177
templates 7-8
tender 258
test-cycle 191
tested 72
tester 77
testing 26, 54, 71-72, 98, 102, 123, 153, 186, 189, 249
themes 237
themselves 244
therefore 258
theyre 144
things 124, 180, 188, 219, 255
thinking 75, 105
thorough 224
thoroughly 68
thought 199, 234
through 68, 74, 84, 93, 103, 111
throughout 1, 26, 55, 113

time-based 193
time-bound 34
timeframe 182
timeframes 95
timeline 179, 224, 241
timely 23, 245, 257
timetable 167
together 70, 107, 123, 264
tolerance 145
tolerated 161
tomorrow 131
tomorrows 125
topics 142
top-level 70
touched 147
toward 85, 221
towards 59, 136, 138-139
traceable 245
traced 153
tracked 21, 119, 159, 196
tracking 22, 28, 145, 211
tracks 81
trademark 1
trademarks 1
trained 23, 27, 33, 54, 58, 186, 250
training 19, 71, 82, 86, 90, 117, 127, 153, 185, 194, 217, 220, 237-238, 257
Transfer 11, 20, 37, 47, 64, 78, 81, 86, 90, 129, 185, 251
transition 76, 83, 117
translated 23
trends 16, 126, 186, 208
triggers 185
trouble 82
trying 7, 106, 188, 228
two-page 173
typical 218
typically 55
uncovered 147
undergo 94, 109
underlying 70, 101
underruns 192
understand 32, 68, 144-145, 195, 233, 236, 249
understood 96, 146

unexpected   57, 61
unique 106, 123
Unless 7
unpriced   156
unresolved   169
upcoming   88
update   176, 262
updated   8-9, 167, 222, 255
updates   9, 86, 251
updating   196, 214
usability   70
usable 116, 245
useful 74, 87, 116, 125, 154, 203
usefully 9
utility   174
utilizing 67
validate   34, 52, 247
validated   23, 28, 32, 126
Validation   35, 60, 237, 247
validity 97
valuable   7
values 157, 194, 208
variables   46, 81, 227, 238
variance   5, 43, 157, 172, 235-236, 245
variances   178, 192-193, 196, 210, 245-246
variation   15, 33, 41, 43-44, 46, 68, 85
various 49, 53, 58, 197, 257
vendor 57, 84, 86, 101, 108, 131, 168, 196, 258
Vendors   75, 214
verified 9, 23, 28, 32, 57
verify   85, 90, 176, 185, 187, 222, 246, 248, 261
version 24, 81, 122, 251, 266
versions   23, 36
versus 26, 145
viable 154
viewpoint   262
viewpoints   262
Violation   153
visible 58
visibly 128
vision   122
visions 139
visualize   73, 175

voices 135
volunteer   250
volunteers   233
warning   45
warranty   1
weaknesses   136, 165, 212, 254
website   222, 233
weighted   218
whatever   17
whether   7, 113
-which 206
widespread   87-88
willing 184, 188, 249
within 19, 22, 26, 28, 41, 43, 56, 58, 62-63, 95, 99, 105, 124, 126, 156, 161, 163, 174, 188, 195, 208, 215, 220, 224, 233-234, 238, 254, 257-258, 265
without1, 11, 16, 48, 62, 225, 236, 261
worked   74, 153
workers   172
workflow   226
working   19, 72, 112-113, 117, 128, 194-195, 200, 206, 226
work-life   195
Worksheet   3-4, 174, 182
writing 105, 143, 145, 148
written 1, 82, 160, 229
youhave   144
yourself   126